WHO DO WITH WORDS
(a blerd love tone manifesto)

WHO DO WITH WORDS

Tracie Morris

(revised & expanded,
with an afterword by
Robin D.G. Kelley)

chax 2019

ISBN 978-1-946104-21-2

Cover design for first edition, Tracie Morris and Jemman (TM), 2018, all rights reserved.

Any change on cover design for the second edition is by Chax Press.

First edition of *Who Do With Words* was published by Chax Press in 2018, and this second edition, which is substantially revised and expanded, with a new afterword by Robin D.G. Kelley, is being published by Chax Press in 2019.

Robin D.G. Kelley teaches History and Black Studies at UCLA and has authored several books, including *Freedom Dreams: The Black Radical Imagination.*

Chax Press is supported by private donors. We are thankful to all of our contributors and members. You can join them!

Please see *https://chax.org/support/* for more information.

To Fred Moten —

    thanks for the introduction.

To my brother John,

    the first Blerd I ever knew.

"One never knows; do one?"
—*Fats Waller*

Contents

Unintended Preface:
Poetry, The Body, The Manifesto

[This essay was written for the "More Than a Manifesto: The Poet's Essay" conference organized by Dorothea Laskey at Columbia University on March 3, 2018 while the first edition of Who Do with Words *was being printed. It was suggested by a scholar there that this essay might be a good preface for this book. If the academic-y lingo isn't your thing feel free to skip this part. I've revised my original lecture comments slightly for readability.—TM]*

What a great, and humbling, pleasure it is to muse on relating poetry and the poetic imagination to the essay and manifesto. My new book, *Who Do with Words*, is called a manifesto because I wanted to be clear about its advocacy, its subjectivity, its passion. It's semi-autobiographical and about my interpretation of philosopher John Langshaw Austin's book *How To Do Things with Words*, Blerdom (Black nerdom), and Black power. This essay explores Austin's theory, me, my process in writing my first "creative non-fiction" book, and what I hope to achieve in this fledgling effort.

This book was tough to write because it makes plain some of the more subtly worded *raisons d'*être for my writing poems, essays, and now this new thing. Its exposition expo(u)ses.

As embodiment, it's my heart on my sleeve. It's my heart on my arm, bared, revealing my (im)pulses. As my *seventh* written/edited book, I hope it's lucky.

As the first part of a triptych of writings on J.L. Austin (as he is usually known), I can't help but frame this conversation as a trinity too: Heart, Mind, Spirit. Manifesto, Essay, Poem. I am, of course, making up these categories about my work. They are interchangeable and none of them are "real." Their constructions, like race, gender, and time, are human made, and yet, because we act on these constructions and are acted upon because of them, the implications, the effects, the perlocutions, *are* real.

Let's try this again: Heart, Mind, Spirit: Locution, Illocution, Perlocution. Imma let me finish: Meaning, Intent, Effect. Once more: What I feel, manifesto; what I think, essay; what the results *are*, the poem.

These three categories, this three-card monte, is shifting shapes. This trio doesn't offer an order; they're non-linear.

I've gone over several drafts in my comments today and that means tossing and turning, not watching and watching videos, eating and not eating, worrying, waiting with bated breath, pushing the "baby" out.

I think we're all worried as academics: We overthink and we overkill. How many drafts of a dissertation? How many drafts of a paper? What's this draft like? (Boy, was it drafty yesterday.)

In *How To Do Things with Words,* J.L. Austin's permutation of the word "mean," as in meaning, shifts about three times: meaning in terms of definition, in terms of intention, in terms of effect. "What he really meant was…" to contrast what actually happened. What Austin does *not* do is refer to "mean" as in "cruel." Probably why I like him.

The current popular ellipsis expression *"I mean…"* [i] is a search for the middle, for this balance. I realized this morning that embedded in all this is the "golden mean." Between poetry and manifesto is the essay. So I guess this is what this commentary I'm saying now is: between things. This essay *refers* to a manifesto based on poems. The poems seek to concentrate, to articulate the primary human knowing through utterance of the extraordinary. The manifesto seeks to articulate passion, explicating the mundane. So what is *this* essay?

As *How To Do Things with Words* offers, there isn't one right or wrong answer. Only categories that get us closer to what we *mean*. This essay became an explanation of a book I wrote you haven't read (yet?).

During the rainfall outside yesterday, I somewhat randomly remembered the performance Derek Jacobi did as King Lear at BAM a couple years ago. He *whispered* the "Blow winds blow" monologue. He chose to perform it in secret, in communion. Being *Jacobi*, it could be heard in the pin-drop clarity of the back of the house. God/Mother Nature/Father Time needs to *hear* your secret supplication.

The poetics of dramatic performance can amplify *and* silence the wind. Jacobi harnessing this element reminded me of what the poem *cannot* do: It cannot "mean" anything. An essay's purpose is to mean something. In this case, to serve as a "mean" between poem and manifesto.

But not to be mean, which a manifesto or poem *can* do, what I have done in poems sometimes and in this manifesto book, maybe, but that was not its intention. Not what I mean.

Writing my first manifesto is/was difficult because I didn't want to appear to be mean, even if my effort to be meaning*ful* hurt feelings. Will those feelings be hurt? I'm putting out feelers in this essay.

I realize that what I want, what most if not all people want, is joy, is happiness—and one tries not to reach for this at anyone else's expense. This is what I go through all the time trying to say different things in different written contexts (poem, essay, manifesto) rather than other things in live performative contexts (singing, reciting, professing).

Happiness as a construct, as a meaning, is vague, and Austin makes it vaguer in his book by talking about speech performances that don't work as *unhappy* or *infelicitous*. He talks about being unhappy more than being happy, about failure more than success, and I guess I'm doing that too.

Don't we do that? Isn't that what academia is about? *Brooding?* I feel that our predisposition to show smarts is encapsulated in the speech act: "Yeah but…"[ii] I have done, do, this too. Sometimes in poems, essays, and songs. I wondered where this disposition might come from. For me it feels like a disengagement with the body. "You're always in your head," I've said to myself more than once. It may or may not have been said about me behind my back by someone else. When said behind my back, it's outside. When said to myself, where is it?

For my sound poetry, the answer lies *in viscera*. In my poetic imagination, the sound poems' meanings are clearly generated "inside out": Vibrate the organs, touch the ones in you too, the others resonating in the cavity of the corpus, the hidden parts of ourselves. To go beyond literal meaning and into the indescribable transcendent and universal sound/vibration, the omnitexts that stir everything. Out of one's head, out of one's "mind," the poetic imagination *resides* in some way. The body is taken into account with the physics of poetics. What I'm seeking in the essay that's harder to get to in that form is embodied practice, embodied statements that are not constative because they reverberate (and Austin says that this is what all statements do when they do things—which they all do—and that's why the constative delineation ultimately fails: *reverberation* of words *is* doing). Reverberation as utterance manifests as the body's agency in speaking for itself.

But what of the speaking of others? This particular inhabited body is constated as female, Black, short, African American, Brooklyn+[iii], been grown, bookish, dreadlocked. Do I look like a poet, an academic? A sibling, someone's child? A scholar? Someone's teacher? An artist? The

16

flexibility, liquidity of embodiment works in and out, and I guess when I say I wear my heart on my sleeve, on my arm, in a manifesto book, I mean the viscera is outside of me but can it live there? Is it (in another *Derek* Jacobian setting) "Vic(i)ous?"

Maybe *sometimes* on the outside. On the inside I'm always trying to get at that "thing." Some call it "that music." Whatever it is, it's poe*tic*. I'm reaching in and out, up and down, through and through, seeking to reach it.

All these efforts engage the senses, to reference Susan Stewart's book.[iv] When one is not saying words, when one bypasses the heart, if you will, of the constative, one gets to the heart of the performative, hopefully, or at least the arm or sleeve of the performative. The poem is the synecdoche of language rather than the etiolation of language. On this perspective Austin and I fundamentally disagree: Where do we find poetry vis a vis language of the everyday? Outside of the chest, the heart is not utilitarian, but we also *see* how red it is, how it beats.

In the manifesto one could say the same thing, but we usually, when exposed to righteous stridency, say: "That took guts." Less glamorous and smellier than the heart sometimes, but showing the unpleasant insides without equivocation is what is intended, the illocution of that statement.

Who Do with Words intends to speak with a more mainstream Black audience and to make things plain, to tell a few harder truths, and to offer soft-filtered joys. We need both. Less poetics and more exposure, less for academics but more for non-academic Black nerds and others. Socialized female, I don't want to "hurt feelings" and that often gets us into "female trouble." Gut-wrenching is what I would call this book (wrenching my own guts) and therefore it is much like sound poetry in the way it feels *in* me, its perlocutionary aspect, personal effects, rather than what it may conscientiously give off to others.

This book is divorced from the primary poetic impulse toward economy. (I am so predisposed toward this in page-based poetry that I'm considered experimental and to an extent this idea of economy applies to my sound poetry.) The manifesto's plaintive nature and this essay's attempt to ex*plain* are anti-(aes)thetical to my poetic tendencies and therefore this manifesto is freeing. It attempts to assert the freedom of others like me. Whereas a poem can emphasize ways to *not* speak (economy through editing down), this essay I'm speaking now is plainly *saying* a whole bunch of things that are not *implied*.

One way I am understanding what essays do is to go in the polar opposite direction of what I'd like to do as a poet with the same idea. A manifesto makes an assertion, and that is also not what I'm doing right now in this essay. It is not a "force" in that way or the way that Austin uses forces either, it's an offering of an idea as a series of statements of some type.

To riff on the current Black behabitive, "What I'm *not* gonna do is…" use my manifesto to dominate, hopefully, but to *assert in an open way*. If I'm trying to do anything in it, and in this long preface to it in my comments for this forum, it is to *affirm*. The book manifesto asserts empowerment without repression and with passion. I wrote *Who Do with Words* as a manifesto on Black freedom. We do this in many non-Austinian, non-everyday ways, including embodied song as manifesto, like the *Ring Shout*. It "rings out." Although not the etymology of the term, the Ring Shout uses the pacing, the pulsing syncopation, to reverberate body/mind/spirit, and if metal and glass inhabit the room, that certainly includes literal "ringing."

The manifesto reverberates primarily through passion rather than through sound—or at least it does for me in this manifesto effort. The targeted audience of Blerds later includes others of good will. In this second edition I've added this introduction and a few more comments. Much has changed since this book came out, even though it was just last year. The book for Black audiences focuses on a form of performance as essay, to find the golden mean in myself too as a performer and theorist of performance.

This essay is a preface, as I said. I think about being a Blackademic (and here we are in the Ivy Leagues). In the academy the intimacy of being the right person in the right environment with the right credentials usually means being acceptable in the right social environments.

I investigate that construct as a way of balancing the perception outside of my body about who I am. I assert my fundamental self pre-academy and pre-avant-garde core: as a sickly baby Blerd in the projects with my Blerdy sibling, our early meanings and sounds before my adoption into other less-Black contexts that have also embraced me.

We on the margins always re-introduce ourselves, sometimes outing/exposing ourselves, sometimes saying what we mean by what we appear to be as others.

In several days, when *Who Do with Words* can be seen and read, maybe some of this may make sense, maybe. This commentary is what is on my mind, and I realize that I want to *be* happy, to convey happiness/felicity, and, as I said in the introduction to another book, "universal love and care for everyone." That's what the book is about even though that's not necessarily what it "gives off." What I have learned as a poet is to accept what the writing means, whether or not that is what I "want" it to mean.

There is a higher intention besides being liked, being acceptable. It's telling the truth as best as one can, hopefully to make things better. Or one's facet of truth, at least, with passion, asserting what is meaning-full. A manifesto.

Here I talk about J.L. Austin's speech act theory through aspects of Black power through Blerd culture. I wrote this book because the traditional academic post-thesis "book" did not serve my passion for the project. It felt too "square." So instead, I'm creating three books: One on heart (this first one), one for mind (the second one), and one for spirit (the more open-ended third).

The first book embodies through metaphorical visceral symbol: the heart. The heart is the core of the manifesto.

Looking outside myself I again considered writings by two Black poets: the *Abomunist Manifesto* by Bob Kaufman and *African Signs and Spirit Writing* by Harryette Mullen. One's a "poem" and one's an "essay," but I feel that they both reflect the best that manifestos can be because they both convey passion in speaking truth to power, with wry wit on top of everything, something I cannot claim, but aspire to.

Almost all our work, as Black poets, as marginalized people, is political because our embodiment makes these words mean particular things, they inhabit us and reflect us and therefore embody our particular situation: That is, we are affirming ourselves to ourselves while simultaneously being "forced"—that word again—to prove our fundamental human nature, our existence, to others, unfortunately. What a waste of time to have to prove one's humanity in order to live. A necessary burden. It is always being questioned by those who have more "say": Do we exist as *people*? "*Should* we?" some query.[v]

And now I leave you: My musings (and I do defer to my Muse), irrespective of form, affirm our light, goodness, humanity in all utterances and ways of being, and reframing Malcolm X a little, here in Harlem, all *means* being necessary.

— Tracie Morris,
Columbia University, March, 2018

Who Do with Words: Intro

When someone says something is obvious or easy,[vi] it usually isn't. That's about as true as Br'er Rabbit *begging* not to be thrown into the briar patch or "I'm not a racist but…" We know whatever comes next will likely contradict what was initially claimed. Whether it's clever, deceptive, resilient, passive-aggressive, aggressive, phony, or naïve, the "simple statement" isn't always simple. Just as "country bumpkins" are usually the best con artists because people underestimate them,[vii] what we think we *know* can be the thing that likely "hangs us up the most."[viii]

The British philosopher J.L. Austin (1911–1960) investigates everyday language as a form of performance. His writing is clever, complex, vexing, anything but simple. His ideas approach foundational notions of regular, ordinary language that make you think about what utterances do in a deeper way. His style can seem impenetrable but his ideas are clear, relatable, and reveal much about the human condition. Nowadays, when words themselves seem to have been radically stripped of meaning (including official political missives, as George Orwell forewarned), it is even more important to think about how things are done with words and what words do when we engage them.

I thought I'd take a crack at writing something that explains one way I'm approaching the importance of Austin's work and how his theory resonates with what is important about the *value* of words. I wanted to figure him out on my terms and bring folks in who primarily use everyday language (non-academics). In this way, I'm also using footnotes as asides, jokes, reframing, tonal shifts, and hyperlinks.[ix] I hope I can make a convincing assertion here about why his ideas remain timeless and timely by positioning them in ways that matter. I do this because his ideas about speech acts, words, and how they work, can be related to other ideas and actions that have long mattered to me and people like me. I hope you see something in this book that encourages you to look into his text. Austin can seem intimidating if you're not used to his lingo but once you get into it, he reveals humor, brilliance, curiosity, humanity. He *cares* about language and the regular people who use it. The language of everyday people.[x]

Despite his focus on everyday speech, as any great art/scholarship, he inspires renowned contemporary philosophers of his age and others (including Judith Butler, Shoshana Felman, Eve Sedgwick, Jacques Derrida, John Searle) to approach his theories and reframe them. I haven't seen an extensive approach to his theory from an Afrocentric perspective. I've written this book to add to the discourse on his important ideas. His analysis of language can affirm everyone and help us all understand and value this living, growing entity called "language." It therefore can perform as an empowering platform, specifically for Black power.[xi]

When I first encountered his text in 2002, I noted the dearth of consideration in applying his work to people of color and particularly to Black folks. I know everyone can't be "everything" to everyone but the absence of Black references by Austin is something I picked up (maybe that was for the best but we'll never know…). There are also other categories of people, especially artists such as poets and actors and their art forms, that he explicitly does not incorporate into his theory (and explains why they are *not* in his theory). Since I was getting my hackles up about this, I decided to stop complaining about him and took it upon myself to start working with his ideas "outside the box" and in these regards. I'll discuss these topics more in the other two Austin books I'm working on (see the Preface).

I believe that Austin's work can be applied in a myriad of new and exciting ways. I hope to do him justice as well as give some justice to folks like me in this little commentary. I was encouraged to develop my Austin projects by three legendary, wonderful "grown" Black wordsmiths and thinkers who've changed the world with their work: poet Amiri Baraka, theorist Stuart Hall, and novelist Samuel R. Delany. I'm also indebted to Fred Moten, who introduced me to Austin's ideas in his 2002 graduate class. All four of these Black men know/knew Austin's work and specifically encouraged me to continue my application of his ideas. Their support, even if it was just a brief aside, kept me going forward with these ideas long after I wrote my academic dissertation in 2006. That dissertation was chaired, as was my comprehensive exams on Austin, by theorist, philosopher Dr. José Esteban Muñoz.[xii] Dr. Muñoz made this book and the two others forthcoming in this "triptych" possible.

This book definitely does not "diss": it riffs, just as the title of this missive riffs off of the title of Austin's most well-known book. I want to approach my first book on Austin with my heart on my sleeve, being angry and confrontational sometimes, hopeful at other times. (My fundamental perspective is optimistic—I hope that comes through). I'm approaching this text as non-linear, in a storytelling way. I had the luxury of coming at this a little differently than the standard essay because my publisher (Charles Alexander at Chax Press) has given me lots of room to "play." The press specializes in innovative writing, so I didn't feel confined by how I managed the material. It's "free prose" (rather than "free verse").

I also approach this writing less conventionally because I tend to "fan out" in my thinking and not just ponder in a straight line. I'm an experimental poet and like thinking about stuff in unusual ways. I'm riffing off *Austin,* explicitly, in that way too: He backtracks, questions, revisits, and revises his theory *within the book itself.* I am, of course, not replicating his voice in any of these ways but trying to "feel him out" in appreciation of his wordplay. My perspective is to start out with some of the "difficult" relationships to language that we, as humans, have (and therefore have with each other), coming from my point of view of who I am at this moment. Therefore I use specific words and "total speech environments" that have strong riptides in our social currents. I use Austin's tools to better understand what they are "doing."

***

Although obscure for the general public, even the well-read general public, J.L. Austin is renowned among scholars for further developing, in his own way, the philosophical idea that everyday speech (speech acts) are types of performance. He begins his most famous collection of lectures, *How To Do Things with Words* (Harvard University Press, 1962, hereafter *HTDT*), by making a distinction between words that "describe" (convey facts, information) and words that "do" (give commands, insult, suggest, play, etc.). Long theory short, as the book continues he moves away from these two categories and breaks down *speech acts* into three categories: locution, illocution, and perlocution (words-phrases-actions that mean something, those that have a specific intention for being said, and those that have an effect on the person who receives them).

In my first attempt to "get" his work, I thought: Austin starts out straight-up hustling us, he fakes us out. I still feel this way. His two-card, later three-card, monte style, starting from his first sentence ("What I shall have to say here is neither difficult nor contentious; the only merit I should like to claim for it is that of being true, at least in parts."), is to suggest that what he has to say isn't difficult (it is) or contentious (he's contentious with himself), and he questions the true/false dichotomy—but it's also true that what he is engaging with is natural, regular, and everyday (our routine speech). He gives us this connection between the language we regularly speak and ourselves. What he does *not* give is a straightforward way to understanding what we already know. He brings an extraordinary insight into how we use ordinary language. He complicates things because ideas, even regular ideas and ways of speaking them, are complicated. It takes a lot of gears to make language work, even if we consider it an innate ability. Language can be considered differently in different categories depending on what is intended, what is meant, and how the language is understood by the receiver. This becomes obvious once he relays these concepts. However, *understanding the implications of these insights* might be anything but obvious. Austin is asserting that the way everyday people speak is profound. In this text I try to engage a few of his overarching thoughts to remind us/myself of what utterances offer: A deep appreciation of the human condition, one aspect among many of human *beingness*.

For those whose *humanness has been questioned* (here my focus is on people of the African diaspora[xiii]), our understanding of, and reconfiguration of, utterances as performance has often been used *by us* to make ourselves *free*.

In order to get to this way of thinking about Austin's philosophy as a lens for Black freedom, I first had to get beyond the idea that he wasn't really interested in talking about poetry. This is because *I* assert that Black people (as all people do) create language that is freeing in a poetic way as part of my conceptual understanding and practice. To get this concept I had to first figure out how to engage Austin's theories *with* poetry since he steadfastly refused to focus on it. Austin asserts that poetic language isn't the priority and it's basically a *derivative* of "real talk," the everyday speech we use. Poetry is my thing though! So already, out the gate (I was mad at him!), I had to clap back "from jump."[xiv] I realized I had to first think about *my* relationship to poetry and language more deeply *just so I could argue with him for real.*[xv]

Where our disagreement starts is, as the comedy routine goes, "Who's on first?"[xvi]

***

Austin's "dismissal" only works in a certain order: It presumed that everyday speech was the first thing folks said when humans started speaking and poetry is some sort of "flourish" that came after ordinary language use. However, the roots of the performative utterances for humankind are *not* utilitarian everyday speech. People originally *uttered*, and were motivated to frame thoughts through utterances, as attempts to speak of/speak to/speak *as* the extraordinary, the unexplainable, the divine (depending on cultural interpretation). The need to speak at the dawn of humanity is a variation of "What Hath God Wrought?"[xvii] Utterances originate in our human need to respond to something beyond our imagining. (More on this in a bit.)

Speaking of the metaphysical, in the many legends surrounding initiations from one state/status/being to another, there is often a road that gets us to the crossroads, the portal, the next phase. We see this concept, especially in the rational "West," played out in fantasy, fiction, pretend.

For almost every speculative literature platform, the road to and from, changes in status, meaning, and the development of the self (often framed as the hero's "quest") are deceptive. The challenge(s) in his quest (almost always a "he") can be random (or seem random) or be a deliberate obstacle placed to aid in the hero's growth. (An example of the obstacle is the poppy field in the *Wizard of Oz*. They were put in that path to get strung out! They minding their business but got caught up in that field of dreams…[xviii]) The significance of the utterances by the characters as well as the symbolic images in fantasy stories (usually while they discover new things about their world) makes magical moments, personal growth, and creates special communal bonds (for the characters as well as for the readers). The speculative/unreal/imagined/extraordinary/poetic and theatrical aspects of language take us *out* of the everyday. Here I'm conflating the application of fantastic (fantasy) language uses. (Mr. Delany's great speculative work exemplifies this type of genre writing that has strong poetic elements embedded in it.)

***

What's *under* the thing? What's behind it? What's *in* it?—This question, What is the thing?, and its variants are what we often ask when we try to get at the heart of an idea, a moment. What's its core? In speculative fiction and in poetry, the road and the portal collaborate to lead us *on*, heightening *perception*. It is not "practical" in its intent. We accept this when we come to these approaches to language. In thinking about words as action, as performance, Austin illuminates something at once obvious and revelatory. He focuses on the language of everyday but the articulation of this fundamental idea is a key that can unlock *all* uses of language. He says *and* asks *How to do things with words./?* It's trickster language. He's "just *playing*."[xix]

What if it reveals more than we think? Is *How To Do Things with Words* a "magical" portal to that (yellow brick) road of illumination? To put words to the heretofore unutterable *relationship to language* that we all, as human beings, share? Whether fictionalized, ritualized, or in some other way concretized in human understanding and belief, words evoke, invoke, create through their existence and the meaning we attach to them, how they attach themselves to us. This has ever been the case.[xx]

***

"The blackness begins, the blackness ends":[xxi] What does "Blackness" mean in this context of understanding what language can do? The unlimited potential of what we say? We are making anew with words too. Speculative words building worlds and we speculate/recreate with this "put upon" text? For the majority of us who speak this language and European-based languages in general, we are born into this text and yet the source of it was forced upon us. So we have a relationship to it for less than half a millennium that is not fixed. What about *before* that? Can we remember that too? Can we make something up that goes back and then further back? What does it mean to be/to become someone through language in the imagination?[xxii] Is the performance of *all* words as fluid as "swing" going, in this case, from noun back to (another) verb?[xxiii] Thinging vs. doing (describing an *object* vs. the subject performing something through language) is an idea that's been at the crux of who we are and lately, say the last 400 years or so, *if* we are. And yet, the obvious answer to "is you is or is you ain't?" isn't obvious to everybody.[xxiv] The hybridity in the range of Black (and other) creole languages, draws on the recall, recollection, and recombination of ways of being and knowing that underpin Black speech and Black imagination now and back then. If it didn't, we wouldn't sound different than anyone else wherever we are—every one of us, all the time and everywhere, not just when code-switching. Those old voices, ideas, constructs are in the poetics of Black speech, whether or not we're conscious of those language apparitions, those "dust tracks on a road."

***

Seeing/saying the "unseen"[xxv] (Who you gonna believe? Me?—or your
own lyin' eyes?) is how "we" get/got/git through and so that's in here
too: When I came to J.L. Austin in Fred Moten's graduate class at NYU
in 2002, I was like "Who dis?" (not Fred). Austin either absented those
I hold near and dear (Black people in general), or explicitly said those
I hold near and dear weren't his priority (poets, artists, theater folks,
basically dramatics and carnies of all types—except the stagehands[xxvi]).
So at first I just wrote him off, as I've said:…like his set-ups in *HTDT*,
I keep coming back to the beginnings. My beginnings with him, but
also where I think the beginning *is:* The beginning of humanity and the
beginning of humankind's relationship to language (that is fundamentally
poetic). To me, it was like starting a book from the middle. And, as I
mention throughout, I'm not alone in this.

31

Even if one has a different perspective on the origins, the thing is, I
was offended by the absences. My whole sense of self lived in the parts
he skipped over. Because I was really angry about this, I harrumphed
my way through the book—lucky it was the basis of the whole class,
otherwise I may not have dealt with it at all. As it so happens, he didn't let
me get away that easily. We had to work it out. In other words, I had to
engage my imagination with *him*, despite my very righteous indignation.

***

Trickster—ish.

Once I stopped being defensive at Austin, received his ideas—once I got
into his text—it was the same as befriending any outsider. I was used to it,
born and bred in this eclectic (New York) city, as many city dwellers *do*.[xxvii]

Austin out there talkin' *strange*. Despite the back and forth, I can just tell you what he makes *me* write. I love him, his work. I was mad at him so much that first semester I read him, I should've known he was the philosophical "one" (as far as my standard education goes). Later, when I first heard his voice on tape, after my shaking hands hit "play" on the recording at the British Library in London in one of their private listening rooms, I wept[xxviii] (Hey, don't judge me in my feelings![xxix]), his voice evoking a performative utterance from the/another body. The thumbnail: Austin sets up the premise that words don't simply describe, they *do* things. For example, if, back in the day, someone says: "Those kicks are fresh." They're not just noting that your shoes are new. The person is not just describing the quality of your sneakers. The statement is a compliment. Simple, right? An interesting idea, no? I mean, we know this once someone says it but I never really thought about that sentence *doing* more than one thing until he brought it up and separated those ideas.

Let's say someone says: "Your face is beat to the gods!" That isn't just a description. You get the idea. So Austin leads us down this road for a bit and then backtracks. He's like: "I could be wrong…" Even when someone says something that seems like a neutral description: "These are the new Air Jordans." or "We're going to Junior's for cheesecake." or "They just opened up a Starbucks where the old head shop was back in the day." These descriptors not only describe, they perform something. In these three cases, the performance could be, depending on the speaker: "You're going to have to give up those kicks[xxx]" or "This is to underscore that Brooklyn is the best borough for said dessert" or "There goes the neighborhood. I'm going to have to move because the rent's about to be too damn high." There's nothing neutral or purely descriptive about anything anyone says. It's all "loaded" and meaningful on multiple levels and varies depending on: if it makes sense, what the person's intention was in saying it, how the listener *interpreted* what was being said. (These three components, as we all know, can be completely different things even if everyone hears the same thing being said.)

Now, I could write a book (or, say, a dissertation) just on his use of everyday speech and Black vernacular. That would be a lot and a handful. But fate has blessed/cursed me to see things artistically and experimentally 24/7. I couldn't let Austin "off the hook" theoretically by staying in "his" lane. I wanted to "merge traffic."

***

I keep being in my feelings: Austin's work is meaningful and *useful* beyond its application to everyday speech. It jumpstarted my imagination in a way that I apply this inspired philosophy to poetry, to fantasy, to various ways of seeing. Why not? I come from a culture that has developed extraordinary adaptability to this language, with roots/references in other languages into antiquity. Austin is playing with words and is also doing something very sincere. He's taking seriously the speaking of everyday people. We share this commitment, this interest beyond the established, the insider, the elite. He certainly *could have* written a book about the upper-class and the people in it who attended his lectures at Harvard that comprise his book. And yes, the book itself is a head trip and oriented toward the big brain philosophy scholars that were his students. But the core of his interest here is in the way everybody speaks. He doesn't give more credence to the speech patterns of the wealthy or well-educated than to the working person. He's saying we all use everyday language in a performative way. And this is, fundamentally, why I got past my initial annoyance at what he didn't include and I instead focused on everyone he did include—which is everyone who uses everyday language.

I wrote this book about a philosopher for those outside of the academy and Black folks who are intellectually curious but maybe didn't get access to academic philosophical discourse for "some reason." I wrote this book for *fun* because I like thinking about words, messing with them and wordsmithing; it's a personal tendency, part of my Black diaspora tradition, and it's heartfelt.

We find a way to shapeshift cursed words, to refashion the onslaught of words as actions meant to harm. We transform them, cultivating another performance in some meaningful way, affirming, to us, *in another way, maybe even the opposite of the speaker's intention.*

I feel I can approach Austin and affirm myself (selves) and community because it is a culturally ingrained *habit* for me to do so. *He also* encourages rigorous reconsideration/reconfiguration of his ideas in the book itself. (What I wouldn't give to have quietly sat in on one of his lectures…) I think, and hope, he's fundamentally an egalitarian, a humanitarian. But even if he *wasn't*, the language uses he generates, the ideas asserted, have a mind of their own and are out in the world. These ideas serve me through knotty word forests, unchartered waters, in Maroon/Quilombo/runaway mode that *seem* to have no way.[xxxi]

We have managed to make *a road through* hate, murder, and attempts to destroy our spirits. We have mastered this technique of survival and thriving "under the circumstances." This is what we do. Who's "we"? I'll leave you to your own constructions, but I mean Black people, people of color generally, women, the poor, the Queer, the transcendental, the Transgendered, the displaced, the people of unconventional bodies and mind (as well as, of course, combinations of these fluid categories), and even those who have privilege and use it to undermine oppressive systems (John Brown, anyone?[xxxii]); those who yearn (for others as well as themselves) to breathe free without harming.I *especially* mean those who do not benefit from being perceived of as "neutral," the standard (just as Austin asks us to consider what that even means). I'm also including this biosphere "experiment," this open and organic Mother Earth, the sky and seas, and all her inhabitants are endangered because their goodness, the connection of all life to each other, is not affirmed by too many of her humans, this planet is suffering because of the myopia and greed of a few in one (our) species.[xxxiii]

The lens I use, however, is the one *I* see through as a Black woman from Brooklyn, a grown woman, on this Earth now, part of a people who have found ways where there were none and who also managed to make paths meaningful when they weren't designed to be.

J.L. Austin did not write *How To Do Things with Words* as a goalpost for Black survival, affirmation, freedom, and joy (as far as I know). But that doesn't mean it can't be one of many tools *we* engage with in this way. We have made and remade everything, including the different languages and laws in our own life-affirming refashionings. So why not his text? Jazz lingo, playing The Dozens, Hip Hop verse play, are all examples of our traditions with wordplay that we've refashioned and remixed through this language. Why not the theories of this great philosopher?

What I'm saying is, I got something out of his work. I found myself *in* it ("in the pocket"). It's fun to play with words and do things with them. I'm down with that and am typically Black in that way (though not exclusively the purview of us), because wordplay is the judo of language (using its own weightiness as a tool, a torque) that is designed to potentially save—and kill in the wrong mouths.[xxxiv] Words are not to be trifled with but they can be played with. They can be *messed* with. Therefore the reconfiguration of words, as our culture-defining selves have organized/reorganized them, has also been a guidepost to others on how to do it, and we have, in turn, learned from others.

It would be impossible to write comprehensively about African American language use. I'm not trying to do so here. This book is celebrating our indomitable spirit that illuminates the universe, that has illuminated this planet since the first full humans emerged. I find joy in Austin's book— I've read between the lines to discover my own Black joy throughout its pages—and I share the possibility of ways to find new joys in almost anything, as we always have.

Chapter One: "Man, he corny."^{xxxv}

Nothing about Austin's first line,[xxxvi] said or written, seems inviting, even if you're part of an elite culture or class. His voiced RP gives him an "officious" undertone that he deliberately undermines at will through his own text. Yet from the top, his pithy dismissals of non-everyday speech make him come across as anti-art, or did to me.[xxxvii] I wondered if the Black absence I described earlier may have hinted at something more. Is this "the usual," and we Black folks have to suck it up? Or is he being more pointed in that absence (maybe both)?[xxxviii]

I mean, these lectures occur in the 1950s, it's not as if Black people, our voices, were invisible around the world in this decade in particular. Is he implying that *we* are the weaker, derived version of the "real"? Possibly. But like theater and poetry,[xxxix] Austin talks about what he knows he should talk about, and not what he probably shouldn't, because it's not his area of expertise. *"If ya don't know, now…"*[xl] Well, you still don't know. When's a statement *not* a statement?: I'm just sayin', he (probably) can't *call* it.

Austin's home base in grammar (midwife of his philosophical "mother tongue") is everyday speech in British standard English. He makes the case through something that was, at the time, basic. But whose grammar? Us with our temporally-stressed *"beens"*? Nation within a nation, statement within a statement? Who does *what* with words? Whose rules? Whose drylongso?

"Proper" and "received" are subjective properties when it comes to objective truth in language (no such thing). By making this important point, that everyday language is complex and subjective in how it conveys meaning, Austin in his "uptight" way is saying "Hol' up a minute." If one says "Someone is putting a cape on James Brown…" (Austin didn't say exactly this but close, but *clothes*.) I mean…what *are* we describing? And nowadays the most important question would be "Is the Godfather of Soul *kneeling*?"

***

What's *dat* supposed to mean? We will take anything and make it work. It is a global, communal aptitude/attitude of folks. Irrespective of how we are described, we "do" us. We (re)make our own selves out of the clay bad folks have ground us into, trying to make chalk, a dust up. We use it as *goober dust*. Leading from the old school. Bad folks be *funny* sometimes. If they can get retro, so can we: People "feel like" treating us as equal sometimes, means we ain't equal, to them (being all sometimey), much less when they *don't* feel like it. Words do things. They inscribe, making marks. As Austin says: "Some statements were shown to be…strictly nonsense." And yet, they are still doing. Can't sleep on that.

"Talkin' yang/out the yin(g)-yang" vs. "Talkin' loud but sayin' nothin'"— two ways of identifying nonsensicalness, but both "un"-real. I don't *think* when we/I said variations of the first phrase in this equation that we had any references to Tao/Feng Shui or anything like that. (Having said so, however, the depth of love Black people felt for Bruce Lee may have generated a metaphysical osmosis in this regard.) It can mean talking "trash," or not knowing what you are talking about. The latter reference means there is a lack of depth, a superficiality in the comment. In James Brown's song by the title, he gives an effective simile of its meaning: "…Like a dull knife, ya just ain't cuttin', you talkin' loud, but *sayin'* nothin'."[xli] So James Brown would disagree with Austin in that "sayin' nothin'" is still doing something with words. They still perform. Brown's performance utterances that don't seem to have logical "meaning" (like his onomatopoetic count-offs to the band while he's singing) are a form of poetic performance (through music) that still convey meaning even if they sound like "nonsense."[xlii]

What more *is* there to be said? These Ebonic colloquialisms are the precursor to identifying "truthiness." Wishing won't make it (more or less) real. But what's *true*? What's reliable? Is "Oh, word?" a phrase just attempting to verify a fact? It is the reinforcement of the real: It's in the context of "trusting" yet verifying (without threats of war). The opposition to Truth isn't lies, it's *questioning the existence of veracity*, the exploitation of subjectivity as the undermining of fundamental values. This is where we are now. "Stop frontin'." (Erving Goffman approves of this message.[xliii])

We would do well to deeply consider our relationship to language now. While the idea of objective truth on any particular topic or idea can be undermined with the death of a thousand cuts (hello internet!), we understand what we mean, what meaning is, based on our core beliefs, for better or worse.

So I've mentioned James Brown's use of the positive concept of "nonsense" to challenge Austin's idea that things need to "make sense" to be able to perform. (I'll give other positive examples later.) But what about the "worse" side of the equation? How does making the idea that things perform, even when they don't "make sense," a problem? In this era of dissembling, deliberate "messing up" of phrases and what they imply, as well as gaslighting toward the listener/reader/viewer, we're lead to believe that, for instance, identifying racism or stating that something is, in fact, racist, is so socially unacceptable that the bar for this description has become impossibly high.[xliv] The threshold for what is universally agreed upon as racist is *stratospheric* (seriously, a tardigrade can't mess with that atmosphere). Therefore there is a significant obstacle to utter this speech act ("that's racist") without pushback, *irrespective of the identification of the speaker making the racist statement.* Austin gave me some ideas to think through this problem: "Racism" as an identifying marker has become a powerless term, in Lewis Carroll's Jabberwocky realm, where it kinda sounds like it means something—but does it? To accuse someone(s) of racism or racist behavior in any context nowadays is to nullify the behavior and have it reversed (as a tool to indict the person who identifies it), even if the utterers of racist performative statements are as extremist as (Neo-)Nazis/white supremacists. So those who fall (even slightly) short of this most reactionary category *almost certainly will not be circumspect about their racism.* In short, the identification of racism is impossible, conceptually, to *achieve* in the minds of many. The *nullification* of the use of the term "racist"/"racism" to identify behaviors, speech acts, and utterances is a form of violent behavior. It's "disappearing" our struggle to even identify the problem and its symptoms, much less to fight it. This *disappearance itself* has become the *etiolation* of evil's evil (a pallid reflection of the original), a bleak shadow within a longer shadow. At this juncture, the identification of racism/racists/white supremacy also has lost its gravity because the extremist bigots put it into the world now as a "badge of honor." Through its use and repetition in social media, etc., this identification begins to lose its shock value and become acceptable. It is an etiolation, then, of "not being politically correct," independent, transgressive, in their bigoted statements. Because this idea of the maverick is so closely identified with American "rugged individualism," the conflation of independence and this form of dehumanizing cruelty is particularly toxic.

***

I've wondered why Austin used this term, *etiolation*, with its loaded botanical visuals. Why was he repurposing this kind of scientific, biological, technical language here? (Was it the "in thing" for philosophers at the time?) He often uses rhetorical "inversions" in his argument and maybe he found a way to convey it here through an arresting image. It provokes my thinking, even if I disagree with the context he put it in (that poetry and theatrical language are just etiolations of everyday speech and therefore not within the scope of his book). The lack of "sunlight" that results in etiolation is what I'm talking about here: The disappearance and *hiding* of racism as a term undermines identifying it in reality. It's the lack of "illumination" that prevents us, collectively, from growing. At least that's what I'm generating from his use of the term.

41

I want to appropriate this concept of etiolation as anti-racist code/ commentary whether Austin intended it to be so or not. We have to come up with other words, repurpose other terms, when the ones we want are inadequate or made "void."[xlv] One way to address racism is to begin to overtly identify issues, situations, etc. as racist without shying away from direct terms, *direct statements,* and (re)framed word usages when speaking them. This identification requires that the term "racism" is used in the context of power dynamics that makes it possible. Bigotry is not desired, is heinous as a rule, but racism does not have the same meaning as "bigotry," "prejudice," or "bias." It depends upon superstructural power dynamics to be in effect and those dynamics are often *ingrained*. In framing racialized harassment, racist behavior, racism as a concept, and by clarifying that the term, the *identification* of racism, holds an etiolative status now, we differentiate uses of the term by those who seek to identify it and those who seek to hide it. In the hiding, it is voided because it does not exist conceptually and cannot be identified clearly in actuality. So, in a sentence, one could say, "When you say that the utterance 'send her back' doesn't mean you're a bigot, and is just a way of saying that you're just a patriotic American, someone (me for example) could say you're being etiolative in your prejudice, but you're still a racist bigot. She's just as American as you. Send her back? That's here!"[xlvi]

***

More Black Joy through language:

However-esenever,[xlvii] as a personal moral code, I tend *not* to assume the worst in people, believe it or not. I don't *assume* that people are working in an overtly racist (or racist-enabling) way 24/7. I really feel it is important not to live a cynical or defeatist mindset. That just helps people use words against us. The big bad "they" don't even need to fight us if we already have given up.

I lean toward a life of joy and optimism, in a grown-up way, *hopefully*. Therefore, when an individual, a group, a law, a document, and/or institution clearly exhibits racist characteristics, behaviors, or performs in a racist way to individuals or groups, we need to identify this behavior clearly, wisely, to the best of our ability, to be deliberate and *to make it plain,*[xlviii] using the best speech acts available to do so in the circumstances in which racist behavior exists.

***

While *white supremacists* continue to march and murder in broad daylight, they are running from the "racist" label too, incredibly, attempting to co-opt the defenders of justice by calling themselves "white civil rights organizations," "alternative," and "white nationalists." They are attempting to remake the identifying of racism as an abstraction, a ghost, a "truthy" affect/specter, unreal.

The performance of the term "white supremacy"[xlix] as a motive, as a goal, is a specific, unequivocal utterance of identifying racist power in abstraction and in fact. It's also a way of "connecting the dots" of things/ideas/statements that seem "objective" on the surface but support an idea of White superiority.[l] The delineations between *types* of lies, untruths, and unworkable statements helps us to pinpoint what the "is" is, where the "there" is. Although Austin didn't talk about us, we can make his ideas *werk*, mainly because he gave us great tools to refashion and because we're *really excellent* at this particular type of alchemical reconfiguration from leaden dehumanizing speech acts to dazzling life affirming ones. We've had to become these sorts of adepts in our interactions with each other and in our imaginations. So, for instance, when he says that there's a difference between lying about something that *can be* true, versus saying something that cannot possibly be true, this gives us a way to more precisely respond to different types of problematic statements:

"I am inherently better than you because my ancestry is from a certain part of Earth"—obvious bigoted statement (that obviously cannot be true). No matter how one sugarcoats it or what substitutive words one uses. A variation on this type of example is "I am inherently better than you as demonstrated by the fact that I am in the position of controlling you/your group (because I benefit from being inherently different than you and your group)"—How many ways can this be said? It's said all the time. It's the classic American "bootstrap" theory masking certain advantages that the person who says it may have. Even if they also work hard, it doesn't mean that some people aren't advantaged over others. This type of dissembling can be sugarcoated to lose all obvious connection to the bigotry embedded in it. An example of a statement that "could be" true but is, in fact, void because it doesn't take the full (speech act) context into account. In the sentence:

"I worked hard to get where I am. You don't hear me complaining" or "My ____ (name ancestor) came to the U.S. with $4 and ended up buying three houses and being a mechanic and a millionaire" or "You get all these handouts and you still complain? I wish I had the advantages you have being a ____ (name a type of marginalized person)."

What's being performed here? Well, several things: ethnic pride, familial pride, (sometimes genuine) lack of understanding of how a person could be oppressed by being part of a group, (sometimes genuine) lack of understanding about how they may have an advantage by being part of another group, sometimes just passive-aggressive bigotry and/or racist statements.

What we have here is a failure to communicate.

So, by naming myself Captain Obvious temporarily in these examples,[li] maybe I'm not offering much, but I want to think about how we can break down these forms of speech, using Austin's philosophy to understand why/how we seem to be saying two different things when we talk to each other (both within our communities and across community lines).

Austin first introduces the idea of relativism in speech by saying that what we often say is simply descriptive, that it can be verified can with yes/no answers, often has a lot more going on than we think. Sure, we could say: "Is my shirt blue, yes or no?" and someone could say if it was or wasn't. But he's also saying that when someone asks the question, they're doing more than just asking the question. The old joke of the wife saying "Does this dress make me look fat?" (pervasive during the 1950s when

Austin was lecturing at Harvard) is an example of what Austin's getting at. If one accepts all the problems with the asking and the answering of the question in the first place, there's the bigger issue: There's no objective answer to it. In the traditional scenario of the joke, it depends on the dress and what one considers "fat," and furthermore, if that look is unattractive (which might be what this fictional wife is getting at). The fictional husband might say yes or no, but the reason why the joke *is* a joke is because it's a trick question. If he says yes, then the wife will accuse him of being insensitive. If he says no, then she'll accuse him of not paying attention.[lii] The question and answer are, to use Austin's term, *infelicitous* (literally, unhappy). They are unhappy consequences to these types of leading questions. The question itself *fails* as a question.

Raising the stakes beyond a dated joke, issues of equality, fairness, and justice, or even failures of personal communication, often require understanding the framing and assumptions behind statements that do things that affect certain people.

A great example of this occurs in Jordan Peele's film, *Get Out*, when one of the film's villains, Dean Armitage (played by Bradley Whitford), says "I would've voted for Obama a third time if I could have." as a way to convince Chris (played by Daniel Kaluuya) that he was racially "safe" in Dean's home. This statement fails to assuage Chris and also fails as an assertion that this statement, in any way, would mean that he was not racist by anyone who'd heard it. It was also "voided," to use another Austin term, by the fact that the Dean character was a modern-day slaver in the film.[liii]

Chapter Two: Double Consciousmess

How do we hold it together, hold on? In the situation we find ourselves in, we are often negotiating the failure of language in, say, the original inequities in the Constitution of the United States and how we, as a nation, are still far from its promise. In the performance of English (just to name one language), we also have to negotiate how we are part of a society that still oppresses us and that we have been central in making, in its strengths and its flaws.

House of Horror: Edgar Allan Poe wrote some scary stuff. The hairs on the back of my neck rise when I can hear the heart beating under the floorboards, echoing. (I realize Poe's characters simply could be (criminally) insane or part of the author's drug-addled fever dreams but still…) Dude could *pen*[liv] and his narratively-driven poems haunted me and satisfied me as a child in a way Mother Goose and her happy end rhyme schemes never could…no pat answers from Poe, but great, resonating conclusions. This notion in writing was life altering for me: That one could feel satisfaction because of a deeper understanding of an idea even if the ending was "unhappy." Despite Poe's extraordinary impact on my imagination, my life of the mind, and my life as a writer, he was also an avowed pro-slavery racist.[lv] I highly suspect J.R.R. Tolkien had…problems.[lvi] So what do we do with their words and how we feel about them? Well…

***

While I was a sickly kid, wheezing and trying to survive in East New York, Brooklyn, those Edgar Allan Poe stories and other speculative fiction (literally) gave me *life*. His tales encouraged my imagination (and dissociation) from my health troubles. I was subjected to overwhelmingly terrible education systems until high school, as well as environmental racism that worsened my health. So I leaned into Poe's great writing and absorbing, inextricable tales. He helped keep me riveted, optimistic, going. *A Wrinkle in Time, The Martian Chronicles, Dune* trilogy, and later, *The Lathe of Heaven* and *Dhalgren*…these makers (deconstructors) of imperialist worlds, these alternate Earth/space-based cowboy variations, were still useful even in the context of Black power 1970s affirmations. Maybe my mind just needed a break: This was the time of Marvin Gaye's bracingly true song "What's Going On?" where, to use the title of another great song of the time, it felt as though, in its entirety, "The *World* is a Ghetto." Living in a so-called ghetto at the time, it felt a bit much to take, especially while I was so sick, not to mention a sensitive soul, like most little kids. I think I needed Poe (and his intense hyperrealism of horror) and those speculative fiction others in the mix. A psychic split in time, in the temporal order, in my imagination, allowed me not to throw ideologically supremacist babies out with all the speculative bathwater. There was a truth in them about other wor(l)ds, places where I yearned to breathe free. The distinction that Austin makes between what someone intends with their speech versus how it performs for the listener/reader/ viewer is appropriate to mention here. These kinds of speech acts (illocutionary vs. perlocutionary) serve different audiences. Poe's intended audience was people like him (his illocutionary intention) but his writing positively affected people like me (his perlocutionary effect).

What helped me get to an effect that was different from Poe's "cause" for writing was the socializing I had of knowing-that-it's-nonsense of white supremacy. So while engaged in the framing of infinite possibility through the overall genre of speculative fiction, I could dismiss the context of Poe's exclusion and real life bigotry and get what *I* wanted out of his compelling work. This standard coping mechanism has often been developed by those marginalized toward the work of the group in power. For many Black folks like me it is the grapple position, the *roda Angola* deep knee bend of the Blerd. Our ground: "Black pride." Our adversary: the oil-slicked body of the brainwashing by imaginary White worlds where we absent *ourselves* or perceive of ourselves, neutrally, as slaves, *still*. We hover between realms of Black consciousness…[lviii]

***

My brother and his friends are in the living room playing Dungeons and Dragons back in the day when all D&D meant was *imagining and declaring*. You just listened to the dungeon master and *thought* things. Adorable. The descriptive fallacy embedded in a "not real" world, but the actual visual dystopia of our "village ghetto land"[lix] was as surreal as the fantasy roles they volunteered to play: The slow-mo death of o.d.ing heroin addicts physically becoming lower and lower every day until they were seen prostrate, milky-eyed, and blue. Those outsiders that were too far gone for the shooting galleries.[lx]

Just as the notion of transubstantiation helped generate the (often anti-Semitic) myth of vampirism in the Western European imagination[lxi] that is now part of global culture everywhere, there can be random unpredictability of going into "flip mode" regarding things "not seen." Even if our concerns weren't what the speculative writers imagined, they helped us to "dream a world" where we are not only not *things* (as part of our former status as chattel), we are and become more transcendent— and we didn't have to drown/walk on water to be so (this time). Sometimes that "flippin' the script" we did was based on Gary Gygax and Dave Arneson's constructions, sometimes it was our grandmas' and people on the stoop.[lxii] We took the performance of these games and stories and made something creatively performative with them (especially because the whole group playing D&D were Black kids—because we all lived in the same area). We saw ourselves in these stories. We were not marginalized in them. We were central figures. We absorbed the concept of "neutral" that Gygax et al felt about themselves and people like them and logically placed ourselves in these worlds.[lxiii]

The lore of rings in our Flatbush/Linden Boulevard/125th St./Jamaica Boulevard/Grand Concourse/Victory Boulevard references were brass, copper, jangled on fold up tables with a whiff of mobile street merchant oil-based incense suffusing girls and *qweens* from around the way. So what were we doing with words when a few of us also read along with the tales of Aragon? Were we making or making belief/believe[lxiv]? *Who* does nerdness?

***

Black swagger cool philosophy: I never met a Blerd looking like Urkel (but I have met some with similar names on rare occasions). Even nerdy Black style becomes its own definition of cool. Urkel had to have a goofy name, ridiculous clothes, *and* an affected voice with absolutely *no* bass in it (not even *trying* to have any bass) in order to be a Black nerd who was uncool. He had to deny Black affect three times to get that super-"herb" affect. The actor, Jaleel White, couldn't even sustain that herb style in real life after the credits for the show wrapped.[lxv] As soon as he could control his own wardrobe (while retaining his huge, sleepy eyes into adulthood), he was *naturally too cool* to capitalize on his old character.

Furthermore, he could never make that transition that Anthony Michael Hall did from goofball kid to buff adult actor. White's transition from nerd boy to grown-ass man was a bit too cool to be acceptable for "general audiences." Maybe his "diesel" frame was even a liability to his child to adult acting shift (even Urkel could become a "threatening" Black man in the eyes of some predisposed to that fear). In many ways, the strong Black man is still "scary," even one formerly beloved, and the odds are against most successful child actors to transition to successful adult actors anyway. Add a racial component to the dicey mix of long-term acting fame and it can be tougher in the way that racial minorities almost always have a tougher road in mainstream culture.

Chapter Three: Enter the *Afrosphere*

The philosophy of Black cool is that our performance of it *makes* it cool. Even my nerdy brother and his friends wouldn't look out of place in the streets of Black Brooklyn or *any* junior high in NYC. While all teens wish they were someone else (even if that's just an adult version of themselves), the RPG imaginings of my tween sibling and his friends (and me every once in a while) substitute Black cool on White characterization because their regular style, speech, behavior, was, besides D&D references, no different than any other average kid in the 'hood.

Maybe this speculative code-switching was conscious, maybe it wasn't. Some of it was a cultural default, just how they rolled. For example, one of my sibling's nerdy friends had a decent-sized, always perfectly round 'fro. He was the nerdiest of the bunch and socially awkward (we all were but he was extreme). Dude would've been the coolest cat at the party had he gone to my newly integrated, previously all-White high school, just because of his hair. (I say this with experience of being one of the kids helping to integrate my previously all-White high school and seeing how the new Black male kids with afros were perceived by the White male students.)

In this case/context, what is Black nerd culture? Is it outsider? Does it stay that way? What is being performed? Whether D&D or *LoTR* utterances are "real" or not, the burgeoning aspects of Blerdness and the imagination through utterance and seeing what was not "really" there conflates the dreamworld and soulfulness of Black utterance in present time. This unusual conflation of project kids imagining themselves as Paladins, Elves, Druids, Wizards, Warlocks, Monks, Barbarians, magical men (almost always men) in their pre-descended *basso profundo* cracking voices was saying something about being/becoming young Black men. They saw themselves there, together, in the projects *and* somewhere else, doing *and* describing an aspect of their future selves, including *surviving into* the future.

The precedent of this "seeing ourselves being somewhere" emerges from seeing the unseen that is a normative part of our tradition. We "get" that concept. Another cultural default: Dreaming numbers to hit (not lotto and its derivatives, not that government-sponsored landscape). The ones *not* picked by *machines* that you could "work with." In popular culture, in knowing ways, we understand that there's more to good fortune than simply chaos theory, an invisible hand giving a helpful nudge to the universe's dodecahedron dice. The specifics of the Howlin' Wolf rendered blues song "I Ain't Superstitious" (accurate depiction of a few of them) and Eddie Murphy's joke about Black people in haunted house movies[lxvi] peek their heads up to "amen" these deep cultural understandings and concepts about respectful appreciation of other realms. We *believe enough* to know better about certain things, including that there is some sort of other "there" there. D&D was just another "there."

***

"Who do/Hoodoo" and *"Who dat say 'you dat'?"*: Could be Jesus, could be *haints,* could be a long "lost" uncle. Could be the wind chiming Aunt Mary via a poorly installed air-conditioning unit in the window… culturally we have a tradition of hedging those bets. A great example of this type of "hedging" is in the Netflix series adaptation of Spike Lee's first film, *She's Gotta Have It*.[lxvii] In the series, Nola Darling realizes she needs all kinds of help and regularly goes to Mars' Afro-Latina Santeria sister *and* another Black woman, a licensed psychotherapist. As Mom Def might've said: Black on both sides.[lxviii]

***

By seeing ourselves in situations, beyond convention, projecting into another world, another dimension, we get ourselves out of our "strange land." Dying, kidnapped Africans came to these shores 400 years ago this year, using their own "new thought movement," praying for something better, not for themselves knowing they'd be worked to death, for their descendants, for us[lxix]. The aspect of my neighborhood that was a "hellscape" that I grew up in is/was a construction—like the one visionary Stevie Wonder sings about with such detail in "Village Ghetto Land" that is real but also contains discrete sections of paradise within its walls—something more than real in these happy places—as is the case in all of Stevie Wonder's *joyous* songs. Inside the projects, inside the building, inside the apartment, inside the living room, inside the imagination playing D&D. Realms within realms. Conceptual fractals.[lxx] Concepts of joy as freedom also appear in Prince's declaration, early in his career, not to be categorized, to reflect upon the speculation, the speculative fictions, about him ("Am I Black or White? Am I Straight or Gay? Controversy."). His early iterations of being a free, indescribable, unlimited Black man.[lxxi] We are not using words to describe ourselves, but to make, to do *through* words.

***

We remember before. The utopia in our blood. In my first editing of this book, we lived on the cusp of the blood red blue moon: A sky scene for this year's film *Black Panther*. The irony that the comic book preceded the political movement is a mystery play on Afrofuturity. The construction of Black futurity in this film was profound and also short-lived. The beaming, chest-out feeling experienced by so many Black audience members was cut short later in the year with *Infinity War*. It was bracing how quickly Wakanda became overrun and how quickly our Black heroes can fall—about six months after the "we" in the story stopped staying to ourselves.[lxxii] I guess in some ways Wakanda has become a metaphor for the internet, where no one can have the privacy of their thoughts and culture and, contrastingly, can also remain too isolated from others.[lxxiii]

Maybe *our concentrated spiritual power* put that stunning *cat* character in the mind of Stan Lee and Jack Kirby. I'm okay with helping start another community-based, self-generated legend…maybe our collective aspirations shape a version of Whoopi Goldberg's character in *Ghost*[lxxiv] in Lee and Kirby's minds. Who says "Hoodoo" only has to be rootwork? Our ancestral calling, that utterance of yearning to b(reath)e free made visible, was felt by all of America, through our presence *as* Americans… Let's say that Stan Lee and Jack Kirby got "open" and, after a while, entered *our* realm. Anything is possible with words, even the *philia* of a Black world, if not a Black planet.[lxxv]

***

Black Panther performs a statement: He/the movement is slick, sexy, he/ they were controlled fury. He is elegant and stylish. He is the literal epitome of Blackness. That "moment." *The New York Times'* Matthew Schneier's headline for the L.A. premier of the film was: "The 'Black Panther' Red Carpet Put Every Other Hollywood Premiere to Shame."[lxxvi] We almost don't have to see the film (but people did: It sold out in most major theaters in *pre-sales* and breezed past the billion dollar mark once the movie opened). Just the trailer let us breathe a little freer for a minute. This particular update of Pan-African utopia began with the debut of Chadwick Boseman in *Captain America: Civil War,* the last year in office of our first Black President. (With the national election in 2008, Black cool went, finally, beyond the smoldering "best friend" and into the leadership, central, spotlight.)

In the swagger in those too brief moments of King T'Challa (and the charm of baby Peter Parker in *CA:CW*'s universe going from herb "zero to superhero"), Blerds saw themselves in this double consciousness subset within the good guy blond-haired uber-men, and others. We weren't framed as the primary cool in "Black Panther's cameo movie" (I'm fine with calling Cap's *Civil War* movie that!), but comparatively speaking, for us, BP *rocked that shit*. The "not to be stepped to" Dora Milaje and Princess Shuri the tech genius balancing the mano-a-mano focus of BP and his metaphorical, post-slavery traumatized counterpoint Killmonger. The film created a slice of a specific interpretation of what a traditional and futurist Eden could be.

***

However, the challenges to affirming Black utopia, challenges to the ability to even *dream* it, are tested every day. After Barack Obama's election in 2008, everyone's perception of the world changed. We began to see how some of those far-flung imagined happy futurisms could be possible, even if the present examples weren't perfect. *Black Panther* the comic book, and now the film character, was/is different because, unlike *Star Trek* (another heavenish-world Blerds affirm), there was no suspicious as-yet-untold cataclysmic event that *must've* de-melanated most of planet Earth and all the other planets, worlds, and suns.[lxxvii] (We've seen planets with plethoras of all rainbow colors of people except the color Black as neutrally "normal" in *Star Trek: The Original Series*. The closest was the stereotypical colors of the bad guys, Klingons and Romulans, always quite brown, mean, and a bit out of control in *TOS*.)

Our affirming projection in this galactic Euro-verse was a Black woman, our future Eve, Lieutenant Uhura. The legendary story of Martin Luther King Jr. asking actor Nichelle Nichols to stay on the show as Uhura so we all could see ourselves (in the) "later" has been well told by her multiple times. As Austin *could* say, Nichols' performance of this projection makes it constative (factual) in the present—and future-verses of our minds. She made normative Blackness, and non-stereotypical Black womanhood, a statement of fact, in the here and now and soon.[lxxviii]

***

Eve had to start it off: In my recall of prepubescent viewings of *Star Trek* reruns, one of the most singularly erotic episodes was the one when they were all buggin', and shirtless swashbuckler George Takei as Sulu grabbed Nichelle Nichols' Uhura to "protect her." She made it clear—like a sista—that she did *not* need his protection.[lxxix] Then there was another *ST:TOS* episode when Ms. Nichols was trying to get "bad Sulu" (alternate universe) to not look at the control board by playing the femme fatale: She teased him, touched him, and then slapped the mess out of him. She was her most overtly sexy in those moments (those chiseled abs and tiny crop top more than making the point). Both of them lit up Magnavoxes the world over. It was… a charged scene, even in reruns, for a prepubescent Blerd girl. [*fans self*][lxxx]

Already, I was primed for the kind of technicolor inter-color sexy framing Sulu and Uhura represented as part of my fantastical world. (Contrastingly, the forced "kiss" between Uhura and James Tiberius in another *ST:TOS* episode, its most controversial, did nothing for tween Blerd me. No chemistry—not even "forced chemistry" between those two on screen.[lxxxi]) I was primed for that type of Asian-African sexual tension because I had, like almost every kid on Earth at the time, encountered celluloid Bruce Lee.

Chapter Four: Welcome to the Blasiasphere

Unspeakably fine, thugged, sexy, and fearless, every Black person who saw Bruce Lee's portrayals in his cinematic heyday projected Blackness *onto* him. We didn't have far to go to generate this fantasy. His nose was "normal," rounded, what we were used to seeing, his high-pitched scream was very "familiar" (ahem),[lxxxii] that glare he had was clearly saying "I am *not* the one." His outrage at having to touch *his own blood* in *Enter the Dragon* endeared him "as" a blood (as the parlance used to be). We took Bruce Lee/Lee Jun-fan into our hearts, we transferred him into our *selves*. (We were all like little Jaden Smith, incorporating Asianness into our kid Black selves in the 2010 *Karate Kid*[lxxxiii] remake.)

Little Black children cried real tears when Bruce Lee died. We used our allowances from stingy working-class parent paychecks for every schlocky cut-and-paste biopic to flood the market after Lee's death. We claimed him as a fallen hero, a fallen *Black* hero, transubstantiated in his friendship with Black boxers and other athletes, like the late great martial artist Jim Kelly. Lee's undeniable Sino-centrality expanded our notion of Blackness rather than circumscribing his Chinese beingness. He was, to reverse the Elijah Muhammad parlance, a Black Asiatic man, in our hearts.

What helped to prompt this conflation of performances from direct descendants of the two largest continents, what was in the political *air*, was the movement toward Non-Aligned nations/Third World solidarity, the dreaming of equality among the majority of the world's population,[lxxxiv] on their own non-Eurocentric terms. The traumas of forced labor, genocide, dehumanizing colonialism, and the flooding of drugs to subdue our political power[lxxxv] is what we had shared for centuries as oppressed people and with oppressed people in antiquity (including European populations oppressed by other European hierarchies and populations). It's racial now and was pre-"racial" before the newest racial constructions, with real consequences. Race is not objectively constative, it's shifting/shiftily performative (but no less behabitively[lxxxvi] real).

***

The transformation of racial "constative" to racial "performative" often works the other way though: The stealing of creative labor by people of color and other vulnerable populations through popular culture appropriated by the "West," as if those creative aspects were "solely from the dominant West(ern Europeans)" and not incorporated from the work of people of color that were part of those societies. The supposition is that we are not a part of the core of the Western canon. This idea of being marginal to the center while appropriation happens by the center at the same time is something we all knew too well in music and other arenas. The tv show *Kung Fu* was Bruce Lee's concept and was only greenlit by being whitewashed. (This erasing of Asians and Asian Americans continued. For example, the tv show *Quincy* was based on the famous Asian American Medical Examiner Thomas Tsunetomi Noguchi.) What a loss this whitewashing was for everyone. The unfairness of erasing Bruce Lee *from his own program, his own conception,* conveys the notion that what you make isn't yours. I mean, after all, "How can an *object, a thing,* control something?" This bigotry resulted in the world having much less of Lee's artistry and technical mastery to illuminate all of us before he died. This small-minded and literal cinematic reframing is the funhouse mirror version of our re-placement of "Blackness" (and in the cases of Lee and Noguchi, Asianness) in majoritarian environs, whether real or fictional. We had a more equitable strategy playing D&D as kids! We are barraged by the reality of "Charles" being in charge, that the world we live in is not of our making. And so, in response and in liberty, we "make do."

***

Ironically, this same "optimism" (born of integrationist aesthetics we accepted as an homage to MLK Jr.'s legacy and acumen, himself being greatly influenced by the crucial Asian philosopher Mahatma Gandhi) can lead to more distressing disappointments.[lxxxvii] On the one hand, we dream a world *anyway* despite historical justifications for pessimism where we are free to associate with whom we want and are all are judged by our character. On the other hand, we continue to be teased with the performative variations of "Come on in, the water's fine. We *like* you!" and sometimes "We like (only) you. You are *special!*" We find ourselves in Charlie Brown/Lucy territory here: The more we dream worlds (whether on mountaintops or otherwise) that everyone wants to be in (an "exalted place"), the more the same o' same o's say: It'd be lovely here if, you know, there weren't more than two of you without at least five of us present. (Despite the global numerological advantage, we just can't "hit" *that* (egalitarian) number.)

In imagining a world, in making J.L. Austin's philosophy of everyone's everyday language part of the superconsciousness of the everyday Blerd canon, I see ourselves in multiverses despite efforts to confine us.

Chapter Five: That Old Black Magic

"Give me my robe, put on my crown; I have immortal longings in me..."

—*Antony and Cleopatra, Act V, Scene ii*

To put a more positive spin on the quote above than the context in which it was written, our definition of Africa, including Egypt, augmented by the cat-like East African features of the Nefertiti bust (in *Berlin*...), the notion of the immortal legacy of Black futurity embedded in Black performative utterances, the constative *as* performative, is demonstrated by the Igbo Landing story, referenced in the film *Daughters of the Dust*, by Julie Dash.[lxxxviii] In traditional telling, the story of the I(g)bo returning back to Igboland in West Africa could mean mass suicide or something magical: returning *home*. The moral of the story is the portal is water ("water on both sides"). The water that carries us away, brings us back.[lxxxix]

***

La Mesa, in Espiritismo, requires water. A syncretic form of mediumship (I suppose they all are), you cannot connect with *los antepasados* unless water is literally "on the table." The crystal ball is a famous metaphysical trope because its transparency in glass resembles water. The glass is... *completely* full.

From the multivolume experimental poetics of Nathaniel Mackey to the Young Adult novel *Akata Witch*[xc] by Nnedi Okorafor, our own embedded culturally fantastical worlds frame the universe's alchemical resonances. The portal to those before us is as accessible as knowing where/when to look, where it's *cool*.

Tutu: Location and Locution: Cool water, as the Yoruba say, as Miles named some sounds, as the Archbishop is called, as the frilly skirt is placed,[xci] identifies what is above and what is below. Some of it is seen, much of it is not, but the thin curtain easily draws open. At one angle, from the top, crinoline looks dense, impenetrable. The side view, however…

***

One of my favorite parts of the *Harry Potter* series, contrarily, was J.K. Rowling's dispatching of Sirius Black (in the book) through the thin veil in the archway that's always there. The randomness of the act and its unfairness in a place like the Ministry of Magic that generally seems safe (the side view, however…) made it a particularly noteworthy way to go out of the picture. That was *cold*, rather than *cool*. The pointedness of this loss of a loved one, the cruelty of the doorway even being there to slip through, looming larger than life just so some people could *look at it*… Why was that dangerous thing out in the open? It was too dangerous even in that section of the Ministry. Why wasn't it put away out of harm's reach in some alternate, unfindable realm? At least in an impenetrable room of requirement?

Rowling doesn't try to resolve this senseless death: Sirius had been unjustly imprisoned for so much of his life and when he finally got out, he wasn't the same. For a brief time he loved and was loved. More than can be said for many who lived and died in that torture chamber Azkaban (Alcatraz and most other penitentiaries). A *Black* man locked up, then "free," but we knew the deck was stacked. Through a ruffled fabric the endless falling through air: Was the utterance he made like a singular note from Miles? A prayer Archbishop Desmond might know? Sirius, a man named after the star behind the Dog Star, the *Dogon* Star.

***

I feel some sort of way: Falling is part of our earliest, lizard-brained fears. A baby won't crawl across clear plexiglass that covers up a deep hole the baby can see. It's not our nature to carelessly fall. Water looks so inviting and it reminds us of the first environment we were aware of then, through a portal. Unfettered air, though, frightens.[xcii]

> *"Why look you how you storm…"*
>
> —*Merchant of Venice*, Act I, Scene iii

Elementa: After Uhura (and *Batgirl*—Black Irish in my kid imagining—truth be told), the next Afrofem Blerd I latched onto as a wee one was Ororo Munroe. I was immediately annoyed, even as a tween, that her powers were Earthbound while many superhuman men were not. She was a Pan-African hybrid embodying post-Malcolm Harlem women and more, representative of America's Black mother from uptown, north and west of her/our mecca of (East) Africa.

62

Her supernaturalness, epitomized by light eyes and white, charged lightning-looking hair seemed to modify her Blackness as syncretic with White beauty standards but not to us: We accept her, despite the halos of Black women wearing afros at the/her time of the original printing, because we have a high tolerance for the range of Black hairstyles (clearly), and because of the effects of incorporating the one drop rule, even imagistically, in our unconditional Black love. (Less "happily," we also knew that, irrespective of ranges of looks, we were all Black enough to be oppressed, even those who "passed," should they have been found out.)

Storm, a version of the weather cemetery goddess Iyansa (in Brazilian Candomble belief systems and others), is a whirlwind, a spiritual guardian not to be harnessed, the I-brought-you-into-this-world-I'll-take-you-out Black woman force, mater icon. The type who will pull a switch off the tree to hit those legs with, saying *be(a)ware*. She's corporeal punishment and safe-keeper of the incorporeal that makes the hairs raise on the back of your neck. I don't know if that is what Lee-Kirby's team of Len Wein and Dave Cockrum meant, but then again, we were given the Bible here, as slaves, in order to control us. Nat Turner, Adam Clayton Powell Jr., Fannie Lou Hamer, Martin Luther King Jr., and Mahalia Jackson, among others, would literally like a word. They weren't planned for in that calculation of "good book use." They were Christians but did not see *La Biblia* as endorsing oppression. *We look inside and see what we can see.* Sometimes we're given great tools from sources outside of ourselves. I was culturally trained to understand this and found something of myself in Storm's being irrespective of who "created" her.

***

Say What?/Says Who?: The beginning of language isn't the utilitarian center Austin states (but *does not perform in his text*). The beginning is exclamatory, onomatopoetic, divine. The first compulsion to "say"— whether a baby's cry or the gasp at the new one's arrival, an utterance that began as an urge that often releases as coming too (the body explicating in two ways through this portal) is not *planned* speech. It is the speaking that *must* come. It is as fundamental a human need as the inhalation and exhalation of breath. Even in solitary confinement, one utters, not to describe a world but to do, to make one, to make ones' *self through the voice.*

Chapter Six: To Do, To Make

In the Spanish language, *hacer* is an infinitive verb for making and doing. *Tomar* is to take as well as to "take in," (among other meanings). My rudimentary Spanish acclimation was stymied by these particular double meanings. Context counts and many words have evolved shifts in meanings, so I don't know why these have long "itched" me. In my junior high school brain, I didn't understand why "making" wasn't a *subset* of doing and how "taking in" (as in imbibing food and drink) could be the same/similar to "taking from" someone. They seemed polar opposites. And yet, those dichotomies (were they really?) made me expand my consciousness to accommodate them. These two forms of doing that I learned from Spanish teachers of color, who happened to be the ones who taught at my junior high school, were conflated, in my mind, with the range of wordplay that my bilingual friends and I spoke. It's a variation on "flippin' it" in the same way that we were doing with English.

The first time "I tried it" linguistically with my mom was with the word "ain't." I remember saying to her that "I ain't" doing something during this Jr. H.S./H.S. period, and she said "Ain't?" like any Black aspirational parent would. I made the argument, even then, that there was nothing wrong with "ain't" because speaking "properly" wasn't appropriate at the moment. (Yes, to my students, I was like that as a *teenager*, going into the performance of language. Lol.) My mom conceded the point. In my way, in *our* way, I was trying to figure out how to use language to survive. One or two random kids I grew up with said I "talked White," but most didn't frame it racially (because we were mainly only around each other). They basically said I was what would later be called a "dork." That expression was too "White" to use back then, and since I was a "female," I couldn't be a "herb." Therefore, "brainiac" was their preferred taunting term. (Even though I was self-conscious about being teased, I considered the etymology and didn't think being brainy was a bad thing, so I guess this was an *infelicitous* insult. It's perlocutionary force rendered inert through my high Blerd terminology references even back then.) Truth be told, I was just some other kind of chick in the 'hood and got bullied for it too, but somehow kept it moving. The speculative fiction books and exposure to language that I acquired being a sickly nerdy child, and the imagination I seized upon to dissociate from my physically compromised body, were strange in my outside environment. This was way before the flood of the internet did two things: 1. helped people to easily find communities of people similar to themselves without having to work hard to find them, and 2. do so without having to leave the house.

When I was well enough to have an outdoors social life, I was well enough to be harassed and I had to learn to "snap"—to use words (cruelly) to survive. Seeking that balance, in my proto-code-switch understanding, was the beginning of an idea that lead me to a PhD down the road.

***

Ana Celia Zentella, a professor of Black and Puerto Rican Studies (as it was then called) at Hunter College, was the first person to introduce me to the idea of code-switching in a formal way, and the first person to use it academically, yet meaningfully, as part of a community I *knew*. The experience of taking a course with her validated the language use that I heard around me all the time. The fact that it was a college setting helped to make it even more "official" for me.

The conflation of words, meanings, the Africanisms and multiethnic sounds of English in New York, generate something new, taking it/ making it not just language but of sonic etymology as well as a path toward a phonemic, colored futurism I'll explain in a moment.

For my mom's generation, the Spanish focus was Cuban (one of my great-aunts was a Batista-era showgirl in Cuba so it was a familial reference too) and the "White" New York influence was primarily Irish Catholic (nuns and other Irish Catholics were major ethnic presences in the local civil service systems, including hospitals and schools in Brooklyn).

For my generation, the majority of Spanish speakers in my sphere were also Caribbean, Puerto Rican, and the main "White" influence via local civil service, including schools and hospitals, was mostly diaspora Jewish. (There was, of course, some overlap among groups.) My brother and I have slightly different accents than my mother and her siblings even though we're all from Brooklyn and lived in the same house. (I won't even get into how the other boroughs have different amalgamated New York accents on top of all these factors.) One of the reasons my sibling and I have different intonations than the generation before (besides the influxes of different numbers of proximate European immigrants into New York public service sector jobs) could be because both us kids were in more racially integrated environments in high school and were exposed to more variety in sounds across the board (but they are all New York City sounds).

By whatever origins, my Brooklyn accent gets heavier the more frank and down home I become, with the code-switching and early Hip Hop slang in that mix. It's a typical scenario of diverse populations, but I think it's still funny how big the shift can be. I even notice my own accent when it gets that thick. There's the literal meaning of what I'm saying and then there's the meaning that underscores something else, like location and generation, that's built into *how* something's said when it's sounded. This goes beyond "making sense" and into another way of "making meaning." As a frequent international traveler, vocalist, and actor, I know how to adjust my voice for different speech environments, but still…that Brooklyn accent will kick in "with the quickness," and depending on the situation, certain colors become more pronounced. Which performance is real? All of them. Austin might say: Why do you even *ask*?

In 2002, as a grad student, I gave a talk on the term "Yo." It's one of those words that I recall as it was being (re)born in a new way in New York. Because I have always been a word nerd, I noticed when people I knew started saying it. When there was a critical mass of Puerto Ricans in my neck of the woods, the word "yo" just sounded like any of the other Spanish words I didn't understand. Then there was a change and I started hearing Black folks who weren't native Spanish speakers say it. When they/we said it, it wasn't the Spanish word for "I," it was an address calling to *you*. So in my mind, it went from "you" (the people saying a word unknown to me that identified the speaker as another person) to a term that brought everyone in, to "us." Someone saying "yo" in this way was including someone else in the conversation. "Yo" meant: "I'm calling to/addressing you." The word now connected us, personally and generally, in our neighborhoods, to each other.[xciii]

Chapter Seven: Pop Culture Tropes: Ain't We Lucky We Got 'Em?

Good Times: Growing up in the NYC 1970s, I remember lots of junkies and I remember Hip Hop. The decimation of our communities during the implosive riots after Martin Luther King Jr.'s murder and the rage of overt political conservatism inside and out of government killing his dreams, manifested in the stubborn hope and descriptive-performative despair in early Hip Hop recordings like "The Message" by Grandmaster Flash and the Furious Five. But the enduring power of what would become a seismic shift in the landscape of "ordinary language" and performative utterances started with what was thought to be a novelty recording at the time, "Rapper's Delight" by the Sugarhill Gang, built upon the sound and especially the bass in the rhythm section of the recording "Good Times" by the band Chic. Complimentarily, the television show *Good Times*, created by Norman Lear, Mike Evans, and Eric Monte, started out as a presentation of working-class Black aspiration/utopia through the lenses of Black power, Black art, Black beauty, and racism-generated poverty in Chicago projects that mirrored my own.

Good Times later became a dystopic minstrel show based on writing/production changes that seemed, to us, to fear this honest down-home Black power. In the revised construction, there was never a way out for the Evanses, and all the inherent glamour and acting skills of Ja'Net DuBois, Esther Rolle, and Bern Nadette Stanis wouldn't change this depressing fact. The show became our *Waiting for Godot*, a purgatory of suffering with no end in sight. Barely bread and too much circus. As the saying goes: "They won't let us be great."

Singer/actor Ralph Carter really was very similar to his fictional character Michael Evans as a kid in the show: He became a Black and Puerto Rican Studies student at Hunter College, including working with the great historian John Henrik Clarke. Ralph's a Brooklynite and a sweetheart, whom I regularly run into, sometimes with his elegant mom in "the BK." Little Mike Evans, his character, wanted to be free and saw to it that he was going to get as close as possible through his own Black empowerment.[xciv]

The fictional kid Michael Evans was never satisfied with the status quo even though he loved his family. Michael was too young to implode in riots, prison, or gangs. His big brother, the age-appropriate "JJ" character portrayed by Jimmie Walker, could've been involved in "the struggle," but he was creative and not really an activist. His art remained a touchstone of embodied Black desire for love, romance, sex, creativity, and freedom in Black spaces.[xcv] It could not be anything less because of the extraordinary visual artist Ernie Barnes, whose work stood in for the JJ character's paintings.

However, the character of JJ himself, as a "Junior" to James Evans, portrayed by the beautiful and powerful actor John Amos, became a caricature of Black pride. The Black talk/AAVE/Ebonics naturalistic speech became a punch line and the primary utterance that the show became known for. The show, twisted off its moorings, became good times only for those who want the image projected of Black people to be servile, weak, sad, poor, and unable to leave these circumstances—a 180 degree turn from the initial self-possessed bearing of Florida Evans' character in *All in the Family* and *Maude*.[xcvi]

The storytelling descendants of the *other Good Times* creative work in the 1970s, the Hip Hop recording, embellished upon the joy and Black playfulness throughout the Chic song. "Rapper's Delight" lifted its strongest rap lines from the great MC Grandmaster Caz (unbeknownst to most of us listeners at the time).[xcvii] It was a delightful medley of scenes from Black life that included comedy. The avalanche of Hip Hop recordings that emerged from that first effort changed the landscape of New York and the world (partially due to the mass acquisition of turntables stolen from stores during/after the 1977 blackout that dispersed early tech throughout our communities[xcviii]).

In both these cultural productions of "good times" we see the irony and meaning of just one term that received traction in popular culture, derived from Black affect and other cultural markers (the tv show from previous spin offs, the music known not only as a song in its own right but renowned for its world-shifting rapping overlay). We have seen the same kind of unusual symbiosis with the two versions of *Black Panther* (comic book series and sociopolitical cultural movement).

Conceptually, whether failed or successful, the speech acts asserted through these two "good times" in the 1970s spoke to specific types of speech act failures and, throwing a little theory back in here, Austin's delineation of mistakes vs. those utterances that are impossible to occur because they can't exist (for example, a statement where someone is alive and bodily present in two different places at once)[xcix] are applicable to the utterances framed by oppressive structures. Is it possible for us to have "good times" given the premises of our being here in America? Should we even try? What if we try and fail? What if we remain, ultimately, *unhappy*? The show's title went from aspirational to ironic.[c]

Throwing us into this void—an endless, joyless existence—as a form of entertainment, as *comedy*, is predicated on assuming that we still have non-human status. This same inhumane concept by oppressors of our "other status" also assumes we cannot feel pain in the same way (with rationales such as: we're objects, three-fifths persons, etc.). Since this framing is also attached to our color, the superstructure says, even if we have the capacity to feel some pain, we deserve it.[ci] It's the assumption that one is the non-human, the thing, the object.[cii]

In the discordant environs inhabited by us Blerds, playing with the fantasy tools we had, we reconfigured the speculative fictions of these worlds. Remade dreamscapes we constructed with our presence predate the Middle Ages' development of un-humanizing slavery, as well as the future that leaves enslavement as distant, abstract memory. We, through these fantasy games and worlds, were making new places for ourselves while negotiating omnipresent, blinding conceptual Whiteness: from the Nordic-Celtic Elves to Aragon. The contrast between them and the dark hordes in *Lord of The Rings* is even further embodied than black and white cowboy hats (red being the outside color, a metaphor of horror: the splayed bodies of Natives). Even the aggregate ghosts, The Dead Men of Dunharrow, in *LoTR* are charmed/charming as specters (being affiliated with Aragon) when he frees them. They are different from the tortured orcs, framed by Tolkien as the color of the bowels of the earth they inhabit. They are the "things" of the story, born to work, born to death in all their "ugly indistinction."

We were socialized not to identify with those monsters. Blerds included. Who are *we* in this collection of Middle Earth beings? Frodo? Gollum? We are nowhere to ourselves, literally, and this leaves us to either identify with White characters in this fiction world or make them Black in our imaginations. As I said, we chose the latter. Because of the dearth of representation of who *I* knew as a kid reading those books, I remember consciously identifying with both Frodo *and* Aragon. I wanted to be the good person as well as a person with power who *decides*. The one *by the fire.*[ciii]

Chapter Eight: "Who Dat say 'You Dat'?"

Our utterances are *fire,* as the expression goes. We put them "on blast." Beyond the attempt at slanted indoctrination using the Bible when people finally decided we could read this language as the enslaved, we created a *new* language with this "English." In many ways we made it quintessentially American. As pidgin was emerging from us, so were field hollers and other post-glossolalia utterances, and the synthesis of African-echoed vocabulary integrated into European languages sung throatily in the early African American church.

The May 20, 1939 cornfield holler recorded by Alan Lomax (available online through the Library of Congress)[civ] is not just a representation of song but of the motivation of what makes one *need* to sing.

These needs are both conceptual and pragmatic. The conceptual need derives from the roots of the inherently poetic utterances that exist in nature at the dawn of human kind:

… one could claim that poetry cannot be the subject of history, for poetry is necessarily prior to history. Poetry expresses the passage from not-knowing to knowing through which we represent the world, including the perspectives of others, to ourselves and those around us.[cv]

A pragmatic aspect of reconfiguring English (and other European languages in this hemisphere) was to utter/sing the songs as coded statements for escaping plantations. We mastered this language use quickly despite the circumstances of our introduction.

The mnemonics of extending collective memory through poetic recall and the transformation of these sounds into others (Ring Shouts, Blues, Gospel, R&B, Jazz, Hip Hop, etc.) is one through line of many. The origins of language are poetic, sonorous. In the reality of African diaspora real world dystopia, a form of resistance is expressing this ancient and primordial relationship to utterance, later to language through onomatopoetics and the extended notes of "song." An example can be found through the Ring Shout performers from the Georgia and South Carolina Sea Islands.

In addition to grammatical codification of African linguistic traits through song, Gullah people used codes for survival. While the impetus for acquiring English words was to understand the world they were forced to live in, they also used that same language to subvert their circumstances.[cvi]

73

In this synthesis of African-based linguistic traits (that I would also say are poetic) as well as coded songs through which they were fashioning their worlds anew, the Gullah/Geechee Ring Shouters are also re-inscribing, doubly-embodying a form of human presence from the beginning of humankind to the reinvestigation of human*ness*. This might be why I could, eventually, see what Austin was doing with his language theory and wordplay (once I decided to be receptive to his ideas). I was used to codes within codes as play, as technique, as world-building, as (re) making ourselves. I grew up with this concept.

The layerings of sounds, languages, embodiment and reconfiguration of meaning, poetics, beingness is at the heart of an endless reshaping, refashioning of the world. This is what we have done, this is what we will always do: This remaking of what is essentially human is the vanguard, the philosophy of the cool.[cvii]

Chapter Nine: Body English

When we *do* with words, in particular, what *is* it that we're doing? What is this sort of embodiment of doing? Does "doing" *need* a body? The pure utterance of onomatopoesis and the overlay/undertone of our essential African selves, as well as our futurist, technologically reshaped beingness (via the origins of utterances by Homo sapiens to the technological futurity of multigenre Hip Hop creations and beyond) is part and parcel of what went before it, *as* it: The saying of the (previously) unsaid.

Saying the unsayable, the *failure* of the utterance, is the beginning of what would become language and poetics of/as language. Onomatopoeia is the approximation of the performance, the *performativity* of sound through the human voice. It is as close as we humans can get to *that Sound*. The phonemic source of utterance is in onomatopoeia. The clusters and revisions of these approximations beginning with the attempts to articulate the unutterable are the atoms of poetry that make the molecules of language.

Trying to make sense of a world beyond our own, the unfathomability of multigenerational, genocidal trauma, the assumption by one's oppressors that one contains neither human nor divine essence, is the empirical crisis element in the heart of this hemisphere's Black speech, song, poetics, and its infinite reconfigurations and joinings. All onomatopoesis collaborates through the body. Our joy lives in and of itself in our hearts and also resists the racist environment that tries to convince us we're not *real*. That joy takes up much more of our hearts, it's the muscle itself.

We resist because we know better *in our spirits and we utter this perception. The uttered voice collaborates in this resistance.* The freakishly dissonant high notes at the end of the theme for the *Good Times* tv show (based in refinement aesthetics in Gospel music and its field holler predecessors) mirrors the shorter synthesized vocal high note of the "Good Times" refrain from Chic that merges with the upper register strings, accompanied by Gospel-inflected piano and a funky rhythm section. (I hear echoes of it in Bruce Lee's celluloid persona's exhalations too. Like I said, he "sounds familiar.") Those high "screams" in both sung versions of this "good times" idea are the responses, the reconciliations of "Aunt Hester's Scream" that Saidiya Hartman references so extraordinarily.[cviii] This more modern version is also the scream of *Jay Hawkins*.

Chapter Ten: I Put a Spelling

The conflation of primordial sound, imagining the fantastic and "spelling," the harnessed abandon that made Jay Hawkins' voice at once revelatory, scary, and joyful, is the multidimensional aspect at the root of performative utterance. The lush string-and-piano-based Jazz rendition of his song "I Put A Spell on You"[cix] by Nina Simone[cx] has the same urgency as Hawkins' abandon (along with shared vibrato vocal references), but she projects "control" in a way that one wonders if the "spell" is more efficacious for her sung character's "purposes." She transforms his glossolalia into Jazz improvisation as studied "evocation."

The bawdy vs. disciplined characterization of the song by both artists encourages a consideration of the "spell" and "spelling" in the formulation of the order of utterances and how they're said. In both the "wild" abandon and "complete discipline" contrasts between the artists' recorded performances, we see an example of Black performance and, in fact, Black freedom, that works "both sides of the street." In saying the "unsayable" through glossolalia, one can then formulate the ideas that are organized in a more standard way to evoke, convince, change, thereby making the unsayable, said with varying tonal shifts.

***

The sayable, however, doesn't just come from those who seek to *re-define*, it comes from those who have the *power to define* too. The embodiment of the sayable, including words that do harm (especially dehumanizing epithets) expresses the embodiment of the speaker who is uttering.[cxi] The meaning shifts because of tone, intent, and other reasons. The locutionary force of the epithet is that it has meaning, that the meaning has a particular intent and an effect. (Again, the effect may be completely different from the intent, which is why one is called illocutionary force and the other perlocutionary force.) The same terms can mean different things because the embodiment of the utterance by the speaker determines what the *said* means—as well as what is *un*said.

In a very helpful conversation with the great writer Samuel R. Delany, renowned for speculative fiction, and a born Harlemite, he outlined this distinction for me with a commonly referred to epithet for Black people:

When I hear black kids striding through the streets talking of nigger this and nigger that, that is the freedom I hear them having **appropriated for themselves.** And it's frightening to most people. But what it says is: The word means what I [want] it to mean, what we want it to say, and we don't care what you want.[cxii] [emphasis mine]

The point Mr. Delany (a.k.a. Chip) makes so succinctly here, and one I had not considered, is that the *failure* of the "frightening term" (as he called it earlier in the correspondence) to frighten *us* was frightening *to others* because it had been alchemically re-fashioned as a form of Black power *by* us.[cxiii] We have "re-versed" the original spell or, in this case, curse. The "failure" of this re-appropriation to eliminate its racist underpinning when said *by* racists (or at the very least by those whose racial privilege revivifies the racist energy of the term when uttered by them) does not mean that the use of this term (or other epithets) as reconfigured isn't doing anything at all to and for us. The intention by the racist speaker is to harm and to demonstrate their privilege. However, the the epithet's illocutionary and perlocutionary acts (its intention as an utterance and the effect of the term being uttered) can both happen, even simultaneously, in "mixed company,"[cxiv] in different ways. We are prescribing how words do things to *us*. As an out Queer Black person, who pioneered the presentation of Queer characters in speculative fiction, Chip also speaks to the metaphor of continuously performing the outing of oneself as a way of reclaiming the clarity of Black Queer power as part of our selves, for himself and for all of us.[cxv]

I must confess that, because of my upbringing, I still feel that this reconfiguration of an epithet "fails" me when I hear it spoken by almost anyone. It fails to feel freeing *to me*, especially because of the mean-spirited appropriation of our creations by racist superstructures and individuals. In other words, through appropriation, even this "fix" we have magically reshaped has locutionary force that can cause harm (it's force through meaning). This is how I have interpreted it. But Chip's point is critical and also correct. It no longer has its intended force when used against us, collectively. We have defeated the original intention of this type of performance.[cxvi] In fact, I have also heard Black comedians use the term descriptively for *anyone* they were referring to, irrespective of race, as a Black variation/substitution for common parlance like "that guy."[cxvii] Like I said, it's still hard for me to hear it that reconfigured way though, even if I know it's a felicitous[cxviii] speech act for others.

***

The indomitable spirit of the African diaspora reframing and overlaying languages, utterances, intents, and meanings is at the vanguard of felicitous and infelicitous speech acts. (Felicitous speech acts are those that Austin identifies as philosophically "happy" because the circumstances are appropriate for the speech act to occur and for its intended meaning to be utilized.) To "flip" disempowering terms and thereby empower them for the utterers (both those who seek to nullify harm as well as those who intend harm in their utterance) "re-spells" a new intention and "unspells" "evil" invocations. We have tied that (c)harmful word up in knots, neutralizing its force.[cxix]

Chapter Eleven: "Get In Formation"^{cxx}

The new formation and reformation of performative speech (and Austin argues all utterances fall under this category, including those that "just" seem to describe) begin at the start of human speaking. The human *need* to embody, reflect the extraordinary, sacred, profound, scary, resistive, and restive through speech/song/poetry/articulation/expression is at the crux of the need to understand and to be understood. This perception-intonation is at the heart of why and how we utter, as well as the world-building this drive for uttering does. These are the fundamental tools we have always used to assert our particular ways of being and doing with words. The *behabitive*^{cxxi} aspect of utterances is for generating rapport, social relationships, and not for specific conventional meaning. *Phatic* acts^{cxxii} (expressions that primarily communicate *social ideas* through vocabulary) allow meaning to be created and reinvented over time. African diaspora communities have generated phatic expressions from the *beginning* of human concepts of time.

In the primordial (and therefore vanguard) creation of utterance, intent and effect are facilitated by a "cool" aesthetic. Multivalent belief systems navigate self-affirmation *and* dangerous bigoted environments (successfully/felicitously or not) through speech or through other forms of expression, through elegantly simple meaning or re-meaning, or by jarring onomatopoeias through the scream, shout, mumble, growl, vibrato, bass notes, and structured or unstructured improvisation. In other words, in all ways.

We have long negotiated the meanings of utterances and refashioned meaning. Knowing this about ourselves indicates we can make even more "frightening terms"—resulting in repackaged utterances that frighten those who seek to harm *us*. The *packet*[cxxiii] is the word and, in that word, the core is the spell, the knot that binds it is the embodiment.[cxxiv] Furthermore, we can create, and have created, new meanings and new effects from either old- or new-made worlds through worl(d)s.

Landing Gentri-fication: One of many whirling complexities in this optimistic utopia through utterance that I'm asserting is the irresolvability of violent appropriation. At the moment we generate expressions to liberate ourselves, these expressions are appropriated, re-uttered, and, by being differently embodied by others, affirm other communities at the expense of ourselves. Then we consider it a drag and we drop it, moving on to the next new concept we'll make, confident in our boundless creativity that continues to serve us well. However, the answer, in my humble opinion, to this conundrum of appropriation, is to *hold on* to our framing of these utterances beyond the concept of "code." In other words, to generate/reanimate created speech acts anew, reaffirming it in our foundation as well as and in new ways. In other words, "Go 'head, run tell dat. So?" We can't just give up our thing just because somebody "be bitin'" us. We must keep our creations for ourselves (and bring back the old "jams"—Gospel, Jazz, and Hip Hop have shown us how to do that well), irrespective of appropriation by others. Sometimes we may even share these creations on purpose, making the world better.[cxxv] If we don't also "maintain" we will get into the habit of running away from the legacy we've built and continue to build upon, often "on the fly(ness)." Sometimes the best evil "trick" to get someone *not* to do something (with words or anything else) is to *copy* them doing something, to try and get *them* to leave their own creations of power.[cxxvi] We can often overcorrect by abandoning our legacies, our innovations, leaving them completely in the hands of those who will use those tools to disappear us and, in other ways, to harm us. We cannot give those who seek to negate our presence "ammunition" by giving our linguistic (s)words-turned-plowshares away, voluntarily disappearing *ourselves*.

***

Truth be told: "Us" vs. "Them" is a convenient foil. Sometimes "us" *is* "them" and sometimes "them" is "*us*." Identity is subject to reconfiguration too. In whatever way one defines oneself, there are markers, delineations of overt and covert utterances we have made, that have *made* us. We should embrace and fight for that cultural legacy, that *spiritual* legacy (ancestral, collective originating embodiment) of refashioning ourselves with memory of our foundational knowledge of self, irrespective of religiosity (including agnosticism/atheism), intracultural specificity, or other beliefs. There are particularities that we can categorize, if we wish,[cxxvii] but I'm talking about the larger concept of fashioning and refashioning in multiple levels and in multiple ways what it means to be human, conscious to ourselves. Our centrality to ourselves does not need to be antithetical to others, that should be clear. But we do have to be central to ourselves in our myriad of ways of being/becoming ourselves.

Chapter Twelve:
From Blerd to Blackademic

2019 is my twenty-first anniversary in higher ed. I started out as a part-time faculty member of a small liberal arts college in 1998 and went through all the hoops to the top of the food chain, a tenured full professor fourteen years later, picking up a few accolades along the way. The air is very different from this vantage point and it made me reflect upon my circumstances.

One can see a sort of rose-colored glass aspect to my journey and if this were a fairy tale, it'd be the end of the story. Hooray! She reached the holy grail! With so many Black women, and others on the fringes of society, barely surviving under the chokehold of oppression, how can one complain?

Well, I'm not. I have a lucky life. I worked at it, but we live in a global society that makes one's circumstances, even one's successes, not solely up to one's gumption. Regularly, I find myself thinking about the giant W.E.B. Du Bois. I thought about his first time walking into Harvard for his PhD, the first Black person to do so. How had he prepared himself emotionally for that journey? How did he shoulder both his personal responsibilities and the legacy of the people on which he stood?

I'm not foolish enough to consider myself on Du Bois' level[cxxviii] and I also did not have to struggle with the stress of being born of that first post-slavery generation. To have the temerity to think one could roll into the most prestigious school in the country, if not the world, at that time, "up from slavery," well, it put my experiences in academia in perspective…

For many of us Blerds, and our proud families, academia seems to be Nirvana. My relationship with formal education started in a fraught way: A precocious reader and writer very early in life, I was shocked into reality that my own brain power was not the sole criterion for my academic success. When I was in pre-k/kindergarten, my family lived, briefly, in a predominantly White area of New York State. I was one of two Black students in the entire pre-k to middle school for gifted children. However, I was confronted with an abusive White teacher who neglected me as a student. What that teacher did, by discouraging me from participating in class, was an attempt to keep me from trying to learn and to be part of the class ecosystem by answering questions. I remember this experience clearly. Never being called upon, never being allowed to contribute. My mother, sensing the change in my usually bubbly personality overall, but especially regarding school, decided to do a bit of "recon." Applying the "good Black don't crack" advantage to her already young self, she posed as a college student teacher observing my class and instructed me *not* to acknowledge her when she sat in the back of my class as a "teaching assistant intern." Playing the ingenue in this brief story, she innocently asked the White teacher at the end of the class why she ignored the little Black girl who raised her hand for every question. The teacher replied, "I didn't see her."[cxxix]

Out of the entire range of Black complexions that comes with being part of the most diverse genetic gene pool of Homo sapiens, genetic roll of the dice leans me toward the lighter brown side of the spectrum. However, in a sea of White children in the frozen tundra of winter in Upstate New York, in no way am I not able to be seen as a Black child with my little Afropuffs. So either the teacher was visually impaired in some way, was a horrible racist abusive teacher, or both (weirdly enough, I bet her white supremacist gaze in some way did *not* allow her to "see" me—how could the little Black girl possibly be the smartest kid in class? Not possible in her limited mind). I do remember being in this class and I do remember seeing my little hand go up and up, and, at a certain point, wondering if I should keep putting it up, hedging.

After Mom got the "I didn't see her" reason…welp. Black momma in racist teacher's grill? Welp *again*. The "ingenue" teaching intern became ferocious. Really, do you think that sedate White folks from upstate were ready for Mom's Bed-Stuy flip mode after messing with her smart Black child? In the Black power 1970s? Chile…

Anyway, needless to say, after everyone at the school got their lives read for the Lord and all attending angels to hear, I was moved to a Black school *immediately* as a reparative strategy. A Black power, Black school with a radical, very smart and advanced Black teacher. Not only did we, class full of Black children, get advanced work that the teacher *assumed* we were capable of absorbing (this actually put me even further ahead of my peers when my parents divorced and we moved back downstate), but we learned about nature by venturing out to nearby rural settings, including interacting with horses, being on farms, etc.

The story of racism and sexism in my formative education and in higher education could be its own book and my mother had several interventions in this story. In an almost poetic way, this first foray into racist confrontation would set the stage for the issues of race and education I've had to face for my entire life. To be a Blerd is one thing. To be a Blerd at the forefront of educational institutionalism (rather than autodidactism), when one appreciates the solace of a curious mind, is a whole 'nother variation on this theme.

Austin talks about *describing versus being/doing*, and I thought about that basic framework while writing this chapter of the book. *Being* a brainiac/Blerd is a form of existence in which one is deeply intellectually curious, likely a hobbyist and also a person who loves learning (maybe about lots of things, maybe about a few things or just one thing). It is a state of mind, but also how one carries oneself in the world. Being named an "academic" (or "Blackademic") is a designation, and with tenured status becomes a stamp of approval. It's Baraka's "swing" again. Going from verb to noun.

In claiming the term "Blerd," "brainiac," or even "smarty-pants" in the context of racial and gender aggression, one is performing an act of self care and self empowerment. "Keep ya head up," or in my case keeping my "hand up," is part of a resistive strategy.

For many of us who grew up in the Black power 70s, we stood on the front line of institutional policies that made integration real and gave us access to environments that we almost never had access to (Du Bois being one of the exceptions that very much proves the rule). We were also supported by the Black power movement, activists, and scholars outside of academia who had to learn truths about Black value on their own terms because they were not taught in those higher education institutions.

This perspective gave me an advantage that I still feel today. It's a core reason why I wrote this book and this chapter. I wanted to write a "FUBU" manifesto in gratitude.[cxxx]

This combination of experiences served me well when I went through a few existential crises when I helped integrate my almost exclusively White high school (at the time) as well as my professional academic environs. I've had practice since the early single digits.

The producer, visionary, and wise woman Baraka Sele once said to a bunch of us women at a get-together that "you are not your job." She's affirming our Black women beingness versus title descriptors with this phrase. Yes, it is significant for those of us who have privileged jobs, who get the stamp of approval from institutions, corporations, etc., not to invest too much defining who we are in the designation. How do we deal with Du Bois' groundbreaking theory of "double-consciousness"? Each of us asks ourselves: *Who are you at this moment? What does it mean to *be* oneself?*

The mythology of academia claims that its tradition in Socratic and other methods makes it fair. I have seen all sorts of people broken by this presumption. I have confronted standard and innovative bigotry in academia (bigoted folks can get creative with their brainpower at an almost Snidely Whiplash level) and if one is a Blerd, it can be disheartening to feel that one's brainpower is not enough or is exploited, since we've relied on it our whole lives and it's given us solace as we've continued to define ourselves in new ways—even when we felt isolated in other ways. It can hurt to one's heart if one has not been prepared. Therefore, having other references outside of academia for self-worth and self-generated knowledge is a crucial tool in this arsenal.

Real Talk from the Lion's Den? Change into a (Loving) Lion Ya'self: How does this aggression work out in real circumstances? Well, some of the usual ways aren't all that unique: Come up with lame excuses for not promoting someone, ubiquitous gaslighting, men taking up all the air even when they are not in the majority in the room, bullying from supervisors— and even support staff (because you're still just an/other Negress and therefore never really have status, irrespective of the title[cxxxi]).[cxxxii] I have heard countless stories of people who thought if they did just the one or two things that would make them acceptable to those in power, they'd be rewarded. Sometimes they are, but when it comes to prejudice, more often than not, people are used, abused, and cast aside for the dangling carrot on the string that they will never reach, the blinders in this analogy being the myth of fairness that doesn't exit—because it doesn't exist *anywhere.*[cxxxiii]

Earlier in the book I mentioned Black Studies in the context of performing artist Ralph Carter. Black Studies originated as a resistive, revolutionary, and reparative strategy for Black folks in particular but for the world generally. It should be normative (as should other forms of "ethnic studies", feminist theory, Queer theory, theories of class and physical and neurological diversity). The world we live in is diverse, that's a fact. We have to be aware of the range and extent of human potential as well as human flaws. It gives one a multidimensional way of understanding the world and all who participate in it. For people who are of harmed and continuously vulnerable populations, a sense of understanding of how one can thrive despite marginalization, historical coping strategies, is critical to survival.[cxxxiv]

As a Black power Blerd in *Good Times*, baby Mike Evans is someone I could relate to. Later, I was also a Black and Puerto Rican Studies minor in college, and my relationship to not only the Black world but the centrality of Black presence in the whole world was critical to my understanding of the world and its inclusivity.

In 2015 I presented work at a conference in Berlin on the great activist, artist, and mother Audre Lorde. In the conference, I reflected on one of my teachers at Hunter College, Myrna Bain, a friend of Audre Lorde's and a fierce advocate for human rights preceding the term "intersectionality" by decades.

Ms. Bain, as an out lesbian, revolutionary, spiritualist, and Black activist, also saw the connections between struggles of the poor, Queer, people of color, and people of all races exploited in grueling factories and other dehumanizing conditions. Primarily however, she was a proud, strong, Black woman who loved other women. At the time that I was taking courses with her, she was so far advanced of my own "project hick from the sticks" understanding that I could not fully absorb the depth of her teaching and significance in my life. It's been many decades and I continue to learn and to be inspired by her.

The 2015 feminist Berlin conference on Audre Lorde was organized by Black women in the city, many of whom were raised in primarily White environments and by one or more White parents, was sweet and caring. With the exception of one or two instances in which, I feel, White privilege was somewhat flagrant and which is beyond the scope of this commentary, the conference was deeply meaningful and exhibited the care Audre Lorde was renowned for. At the conference I spoke about Myrna as an embodiment of the revolutionary practices that Audre Lorde espoused. I received a great deal of insight into Myrna's life and significance because of several conversations I had with my friend, British poet Dorothea Smartt, as well as visual artist Tim Fielder (a.k.a. Rasaan), who also studied with Myrna and who was surrounded by the innovative artists in his Mississippi family. Until my encounter with Myrna, my understanding of Black power was disproportionately heteronormative, cisgendered, and therefore biased. I was, myself, biased in conflating Black activism with a particularly limited type of straight, male Blackness. Although there has always been a known Queer presence in Black communities, as well as a range of gender presentations, many of us "revolutionary Black students" had too narrow a bandwidth when it came to understanding the range of Black power. Not only does it marginalize many within our own communities, but it marginalizes our giants as "exceptions" to the rule of what a Black, powerful person can be. This has practical applications of not understanding, say, the level of profoundness that Bayard Rustin, Audre Lorde, and James Baldwin were giving the world. It was my loss then and continues to be my loss that my narrow priorities had me miss the opportunity to study with Audre Lorde, although many of my friends did. It was the old argument of Ms. Lorde being in Women's Studies and not BLPR as her primary departmental "home" that also affected this lost opportunity by me. Little did I know how hard it was for a Black woman, especially then, to be placed *anywhere* in a decent academic home.[cxxxv]

Myrna was primarily housed in BLPR. I overheard her, many times, in faculty meetings ferociously and unequivocally advocating for a pro-Black and expansively thinking department. She was way ahead of the curve but her very presence there validated her position, then and now, and unbeknownst to us, helped validate the department and its development.

These kinds of difficult conversations and ways of being in the world are imperfect but necessary. What Myrna, Audre Lorde, and others were working through at the departmental levels was not reflected to the same degree in my political science major, or at least not in a way that was detectable to me. As a continuing learning Blerd (goes with the territory), I did, and still do, love political science, law, and public policy, but being part of PoliSci and BLPR felt like two different worlds for me, and at a certain point, I did feel like I had to make a choice between my activist tendencies and my more formal toe-the-line middle-class aspirational tendencies, typical of the economically vulnerable. The activist track or the conventional pre-law track? At the time they felt worlds apart (although Thurgood Marshall and Paul Robeson had long showed the dichotomy I created was a false one). It was somewhat painful too because some of my PoliSci teachers were extraordinary and I fondly reflect on their importance to me to this day, even though I became more politically left and activist than they.[cxxxvi]

Years later I realized that I was also recovering from the trauma of being the first wave of Black and Latinx students to integrate my heretofore all-White high school in Brooklyn. Race riots were common at the high school and no one knew what to do. Still, the extraordinary juxtaposition of the inferior education I had received at my predominantly Black and Latinx Brooklyn elementary schools and junior high school (despite me being a top student in top classes there), and the access to resources, the assumption of excellence, the prep for college, and other opportunities in my White high school, upset me for many years and still does to this day. It's education weaponized against children. I went from being an exceptional student to an average one based on my poor preparation in my earlier schooling. Paradoxically, when I had the confidence to enroll, I ended up doing fine in my Advanced Placement classes and in my drama classes. This does not take away from the fact that my relationship to learning had been shattered in those early, violent, integrationist efforts.

Going into academia as a professor was like coming back to myself (valued as a bookworm) but it was also like coming back to the same issues that pushed me away as a student. Normalizing Afrocentricity as part of American culture and global culture, accepting the range of diversity that is a fact of this world and its peoples, agreeing to fundamental truths of care, empowerment, joy, safety, development, and love, can all work together, but not if one is so wrapped up in one's designation as a particular "title," description, or job, at the expense of one's consciousness, one's *beingness*. Looking back on twenty-one years at this, I can say I have "swung" from verb to noun and back to being again. Once a Blerd *being*, hopefully, always.

Chapter Thirteen: PRN

"I want to be free, free. Yes I am…"
— excerpt from song lyrics "I Want to be Free,"
performed by the Ohio Players

I had a bit of the blues on a rainy morning on my way to the airport. It was June 10, 2018 and I was off on one of my long summer tours filled with teaching, residencies, performances, and a couple of days' vacation. I wasn't blue because I was traveling (I love traveling by train, plane, automobile, by foot, boat, anything). I was blue because my preparation for my trips and their obligations, as well as some other personal ones, precluded my attendance at the annual Prince Purple People party event in Bed-Stuy the previous night. I took it as a sign to finally write about Prince in this second edition a year later. Anyone who knows me from moderately well on up, knows I'm a huge Prince fan, and when a Blerd of any type goes in, we go *way* in. His lyrics and performances are *etched in my heart*. No, my knowledge of his catalogue is not encyclopedic and I'd probably lose the Trivial Pursuit lightning round of his ridiculously prolific published work. However, he's always in my heart, head, and yes, hair.[cxxxvii]

A sexy M.F.er (that's why the title of this chapter is a little bit naughty) like him isn't the first person who comes to mind when one thinks of Blerds: He's fine, a star, sexy, and a celebrity. He is also an artist's artist. This type of phrasing, a ____'s ____, *usually* is affiliated with the greats who are known only or mostly among the greats, but not known as much by the general public. (Austin is one of those types of people for me. He's a philosopher's philosopher.)[cxxxviii] Prince however, is one of the rare artists who is an artist's artist who is *also famous* and was renowned during his life. So why feature him in this Blerd missive?

In addition to being a genius musician, songwriter, dancer, producer, consummate vocalist, and all-around trickster, Prince Rogers Nelson was always *on that grind*. He has loved music his whole life, including the playing, writing, recording, and producing of music. You don't get to where he is/was through talent alone, though he had that in spades. He was obsessive, beyond the "cute" way, with music, and all aspects of performance and presentation. Miles Davis, another artist's artist, famously said that Prince was a combination of Jimi Hendrix, James Brown, Marvin Gaye, and *Charlie Chaplin*. Game knows game, and I am astounded, always, by Miles' acumen as well as his appreciation for another genius Gemini.[cxxxix]

How'd Prince Rogers Nelson go from big 'froed, shawty dork with synths holed up in his room to sexy superstar? Gender blending, being naughty, literally showing his hiney? This year Prince would've been sixty-one and I missed the Spike Lee party in the B-K last year due to conflicts. Maaan…

But Mr. Sheldon Lee represented for sure. As Brooklyn as I am, I have to say that Spike Lee is *the* most Brooklyn—and I do not say this lightly. I do not! Prince was similarly very Twin City and Midwestern (as was Michael Jackson with his Gary, Indiana accent). While Mr. Nelson was very downtown Manhattan when he first came to the City, there's something about his mid-country self that connects in my mind to the cities/towns/boroughs not in the coastal hubs. The kid who makes good ("All the Critics Love You in New York") among the hip posers (who have sadly emigrated to the borough of Kings now) doesn't negate the slightly askew stance we take because we didn't grow up "in the big leagues, getting our turn at bat." We had to earn it through exceptional diligence. Prince was/is a Blerd in my mind.

The only time, so far, that I've been able to go to Spike Lee's Prince jam I was shocked at the range and sheer volume of writing/music he made. How, despite the loneliness he must have experienced through the many hours he was perfecting his crafts (often alone, especially in the early years), he was able to negotiate a public persona and a deeply private one. His is the happy nerd/Blerd success story. All that hard work becomes worth it. All the isolation and obsession is worth it, that one is not only appreciated but *adored*.

While most folks wouldn't consider Prince a Blerd, he is. As is Spike Lee. As is any serious, hard-working artist. One can be born with a great deal of talent, but to apply it over years, decades, to make a choice to forego social constructs because one is so *in it*, is the commitment of the Blerd, the nerd, the dork, the geek. The supplicant, devoted to knowledge, and in that devotion and development creates a body of work that shifts something in themselves and us. The investment of time and care that endures beyond lifetimes. The people who make the world turn.

The day after Prince's death I happened to be performing with the great percussionist Susie Ibarra at the Whitney Museum to celebrate the great poet, musician, and composer Cecil Taylor (who was still with us then). I couldn't have asked for a better gift from the heavens. Cecil was being praised by all sorts of artists and intellectuals during the course of the retrospective and he also came to *play*. Something about being able to honor someone while they were alive helped me process Prince's death. After Susie and I performed I stayed for a while and got a chance to hang out with Fred Moten (who also performed) and the giant Nathaniel Mackey, among others. I ran into them looking for Susie, and I felt the strength, resoluteness, genius, and fragility of Black men, particularly at that moment and before any of us knew that Cecil would not be long for the world himself. The ashes of Black genius swirling around in the air.

I needed to sit with poets to process Prince's death (I love his way with sounds), Cecil's living (I love his way with words), Fred's comments (who brought me to Austin and his way with words), and Nathaniel Mackey (whom Fred and I both idolize). There was this beauty, this artistic beauty, that I was able to remember about Prince rather than focus on his *death*. Being with wordsmiths (and celebrating one—I first encountered Cecil as a poet before I heard his music) gave me solace because we understood the word and the work of word-music-soundsmithing. We research, write, and play in that way as many artists, as well as in a Black way, in particular. That inadvertent send off for Prince as well as Cecil, with Susie (who'd played with him) as well as with other poets, was a gift to remember.

People ask me sometimes if I consider myself a musician (partially because I sing). But when the jig is up, when the chips are down, when there's a joyful noise, I feel in words. Words, words, words. I'm still trying to say something with them, like: rest, rest, rest in peace, sweet, soothing, starlight, sexy Prince. You've earned it, saying so much.

Chapter Fourteen: Grace

…Heeeere's Grace![cxl]

This chapter concerns the idea of grace as well as the person Grace Jones.[cxli] First some thoughts about the concept of Grace: To riff off Austin's riff toward the end of *HTDT,* I'm not saying anything new here. What I'm alluding to is very old and very *now.* Besides the delineations of speech acts and meaning, Austin's humor and humanism comes through in his text, his state of grace. His book itself is a culmination of the love and affection his students had for his work and for him. They *lovingly* compiled his notes and theirs to make *HTDT* and other books under his name. I can see why. His smarts, combined with his self-effacing (and even self-mocking) style, is endearing rather than intimidating, even if it's sometimes confusing because he's so witty and his writing is so dense. It takes a while to get that he's also making fun of himself. He's *charming.* More to the heart of the matter, however, despite all his brilliant structuralism, Austin not only questions utterances, meaning, and language, he questions *himself.* He assumes that he doesn't know everything and that his philosophy will be used to consider ideas that he has not dreamed up, dreamt of.

***

I'm right there with him: Who knows? I don't know what his thoughts were regarding racial justice at the time. In the 1950s there were significant upheavals all over the world: In global anti-colonialist efforts, internal civil rights/human rights struggles throughout the "West," and continued technological innovations that made the world smaller. Austin certainly would've been exposed to these concerns, just by walking through the Harvard and Oxford campuses. I do not know how he responded to these issues or how he felt about them. All I know about him, and his consideration of utterances (specifically speech) in *HTDT*, is that he assumed he was not the ultimate authority on the meanings of even his own words:

It is essential to realize that 'true'

and 'false', like 'free and unfree', do not stand for anything simple at all; but only for a general dimension of being a right or proper thing to say as opposed to a wrong thing, in these circumstances, to this audience, for these purposes and with these intentions.[cxlii]

"Free and unfree?" What's he alluding to here? I'm not presuming to have any *answers* either. I am following Austin's lead in stating that the *journey* of understanding the limitless potential for language as an aspect of performing, of *changing*, is worth considering. In these days and times, where technology and political winds shift so abruptly as to regularly question our sense of ourselves and our communities, it is worth being reminded of historic and futuristic coping strategies on the personal, communal, and global levels. Grace is a coping mechanism for human kindness.

What if we take into account that we, as Black people, are known as "local" innovators and always have been (even while acknowledging that we may not be exclusively so)? Even in our dreaming of our own comity despite speech acts, tortures, and genocides attempting to convince us of the contrary? Then what? How does this leave our self-perception of what we do in/as the world? How do we negotiate the stasis we're in irrespective of whether or not we adopt the barrage of lies that still seek to convince us that we are not "really" human even now?

***

I'm coming back to grace and Grace but first, I have found a new Blerd icon from a "mainstream" source recently: Chidi Anagonye, a fictional character in the television series *The Good Place*.[cxliii] The actor, William Jackson Harper, really sells the character in this innovative network tv show. First off, dude is a Black philosopher and a Blerd to his (non-corporeal) bones. Hello! Second, his character's whole deal throughout the series (so far) is: "Whither do I go?" Without giving away too much of the story arc (it's really worth viewing for yourself), I see commonality in the character beyond the obvious: Blerd Blackademic who's into a specific branch of philosophy. (His specialty is moral philosophy.) Chidi has no self-identified Black community in the "good place" (but to the show's credit they move away from many established racial stereotypes throughout the show, and in the third season Simone Garnett, played by Kirby Howell-Baptiste, has an extensive arc[cxliv]). The "Good Place" is "neutral" and is culturally homogeneous, and self-consciously so. In flashbacks to his Earthly life, he surrounds himself with Black folks. This begs the question for him as a Black man as well as for the audience: "How good a place can this be without his 'peeps'?" Where is he now? Where does *he* go?

***

Beyond the character's personal flaws that help drive the show, I can understand his ambivalence about choosing one thing instead of another in life (and afterlife). How does one truly *know*? We cannot know anything for sure; we have to embrace risk, as Chidi begins to understand. (We hope—anyone who likes the show is certainly rooting for this character and the other "good" ones.)

His Blerd markers are clear: He wears thick glasses and reads a lot. He

can't turn off his knowledge base even if it's socially awkward. And yet…
he's still a pretty cool and super attractive guy. No Urkel overcorrection,
he's probably the more accurate portrayal of an adult male Blerd (with
a little extra allowing for Hollywood framing) I've seen as a featured
character on tv[cxlv] (and, although not breaking any new ground in terms
of the character's straightness or gender, he is also not a nonthreatening
asexual intellectual man of color portrayal either, as is often the case).

The character's backstory is that he was born in Nigeria, raised in
Senegal, and teaches in Australia at the time that he dies. His English
accent is American (even outside of the "good place") and he also speaks
French (and one presumes Wolof/Pulaar and Yoruba/Igbo/Urhobo or
any other Nigerian-based African language—but how would we know?
Who's he going to speak those languages *to*?)

His problems with choosing between things have to do with how his

mind is buried by competing philosophies that give him no clear path.[cxlvi]
He begins to make choices in his (after)life and he also begins to find
the core of himself. While we don't know how the writers of the show
will develop his character, there is potential for his personal growth
through his unconditional care for others. In season three, his existential
quandaries get to the breaking point and affect his ability to teach. He's
in a Blerd moment where academia can't save him and, because it's a tv
show, means he has to cultivate his state of grace without the aid of his
intellect. I feel you, Chidi.

***

If this book were a tv show, this would be a "pivot" to a very (after-
school) special MLK Jr. moment regarding an integrated cast on tv
helping us to understand each other a bit better, especially after all my
"real talk" about racism as a term earlier. Isn't that the way most Black

intellectuals go toward the end of the book? We realize we are not alone, and to make this a "good place" we all hold hands and get invited to nice cocktail parties because ultimately, supposedly, we all want to be liked by elite folks.[cxlvii] This is the point where I say we're all one big happy family. That, however, would be infelicitous on *my* part.[cxlviii] Blerding ain't (that) easy. Blerding as a "minority," even in the afterlife, when you grew up around kith and kin, especially given all we've gone through? Well, that's an adjustment.

***

The Three Graces as One Grace: One of the reasons I like the little interstitial riff by Grace Jones in the song "Slave to the Rhythm" that tops this chapter is not only because she's doing her Black fierce diva remix of the well-known Johnny Carson intro by Ed McMahon (talk about making something new out of language), but because the irony is that Grace Jones has demonstrated time and time again in her real life and her on-camera life that the sedate talk show set isn't the best medium to showcase *her grace*. She's a slave to the rhythm, but that is *all* she is a "slave" to. She is free. She is a free, unpredictable, Afropunk, bold, *foine* Black woman, Black being. Being.

This world citizen goes back to the "bush" when she needs/wants to. She's our dear, dreaded Quilombo runaway and iconic mother-father.[cxlix] We don't know Chidi's parents (yet) but he has a refracted global citizenry, rooted in his African ancestry, his African diaspora accent, as the very real Grace Jones does. The contrast I'm deliberately drawing is between the straight (and "straight") as an arrow, socially acceptable Black characterization and the outlier, "dangerous" "genderqueer" Black person, both proudly displayed in our fantastic realms on current Earth prime, working through sounds and language. I feel affirmed, some kind of way, by both these "universally" *spirited* beings in one lifetime.

But is that accurate? Depending on how one sees these two performances, they are equally dangerous ("frightening" to some) because they are equally embodiments of the Black (human) self, without question or subservience.

The grace that Grace embodies, the nerdiness that William Jackson Harper's character presents, exemplifies a lack of self-consciousness about whether or not they belong in their performative environments (unlike Eleanor, Chidi "knows" from the beginning that he belongs in the "good place"). Grace Jones stopped questioning whether she had the right to belong *anywhere* some time ago, as befits someone of her renown, her *power*.

This "knowledge of self" encourages a radical type of grace that is predicated on the *absence* of existential self-doubt. Irrespective of how one finds it, this is *power*.[cl] It is rooted in knowing that no matter what the circumstances and particular preferences, our contributions to the world from the origins of humankind are an illumination of how to make, remake, make anew.[cli] Through imagination, through utterances of sound, by *saying* we are doing: Making meaning for/of ourselves and remaking as the desire arises. In Jones' life, through her autobiography *I'll Never Write My Memoirs*, she talks about getting back to her foundation in the forests of Jamaica with Rastafarians who have continued the *Maroon* tradition. With her anchor, knowing her *local* Black history, she has the strength to go back to London, Paris, New York, or anywhere else in the world with *elan*, beauty, grit, hard work, talent, charm.

Grace Jones' unique vocal timbre and performance of androgyny, high art, muscularity, and transgression, are speech acts in voice and other embodied practices. Her choices are another way of understanding

Austin's idea of locutionary acts in speech. Her range of utterances, overlays, foundations, and innovations can be dovetailed into these categories with "making speech acts" as a form of meaning, "remaking" as a form of an intention to make. It shows the kinds of slippages that allow Austin to conflate speech with other types of performance. The effect is to make *fresh*,[clii] through the engagement with another (or oneself) in the effect of making.

The mysteries of *how* "making" is made aren't the same as not knowing that making *is being made*. This making is poetic, the source of all utterances. Grace's grace is, to this day, a totality of poetic, performative utterances.

Furthermore, Grace's utterance of the word "slave" underscores an overcoming of the *fear* of certain utterances, through the remaking. Being

aware of their fluidity and potential for refashioning in our own image. This particular knowing releases language's power, knowing it can be remade, honed, harnessed, is readymade (as the avant-garde artists would say), and all the while engaging its essential *truth*. In the current edge of a new decade in this new century/millennium we are inhabiting, many are retreating to social bubbles of mutually assured agreement. Our particular skill at being adepts of remaking utterances/laws/spells *made to unmake us* is the same skill that facilitates adeptness in speaking to people with whom we do not agree, to work through the pain of challenging interactions as a way of appealing to all of our "better angels."

Part of Grace's grace is her fierceness in speaking truth to power and in using her own voice as power as well as her own physical power. *She don't mind being someone's worst nightmare.* Seemingly counterintuitive, I'd say that unapologetic Black power in these circumstances, traveling in the myriad of circles she's often in, and remaining true to oneself, rooted in one's power, certainly qualifies as an exalted state of Grace.

How to create, recreate, remix utterances foundational for human understanding of ourselves (including non-language-based utterances that are onomatopoetic and glossolalic[cliii]) reaches toward something beyond Austin's humane utilitarianism and into a state of consciousness, of *grace*, that can be an even more brilliant "light of the world…"[cliv]

We know fantastic world-making through words when we see them. We always make new worlds. We refashion them out of the sounds we said at the beginning of humankind. We make them out of all the atoms of sounds, even those spoken to harm us. This is what we do: Out of all these building blocks we wail a rhythmic world, create joyful noises, the first thing and new things with words.

Chapter Fifteen: Three Muses — Macy Vaughn, Tray Barker, and Nola Darling

Spoiler alert: This chapter reveals plot points of the tv shows
Charmed (2018 version), The Last O.G., and She's Gotta Have It.

Muse of Practice: Hardcore Blerdom doesn't get harder than STEM. Macy Vaughn came in as the third wheel of the rebooted *Charmed* triumvirate as the nerdiest sister. She is a super-dedicated doctorate-holding scientist (genetics) and they incorporate a bit of science in the show, frequently showing Macy in her lab. She uses her research know-how to help solve magical problems rather than just present the limits of science in the face of magic.[clv]

At the end of the first season Macy (played by Madeleine Mantock) also becomes the most powerful being on Earth as a charmed witch and the source of magic and the source of evil! That is a lot of power! The show is not afraid to go all in with the magical weaponry! It's intriguing how this show incorporates Blerd scientific knowledge as well as magic, including African-based magic, into the concept of the witch (mostly ascribed as a Euro-pagan term and definitely so in *Charmed: TOS*). They throw some Yoruba in there, some Haitian voodoo, some Santeria, a bit of a gamut.[clvi] However, as far as I know, this is the first time that any speculative fiction tv series has tried to really incorporate all these elements, especially in a canon that was established without them originally. What's fascinating about applying speech act theory here is that it ties into this idea connecting extraordinary circumstances with Blerdom and the primordial impulse for performative, poetic speech acts.

The character happily, and coincidentally, connects the dots I'm offering throughout this book, in the Blerd world, speculative fiction world, and science world. (She also was one of two students of color in her K-12 school!—I mean…) She even had to let someone know not to be *touching her hair*.[clvii] Being a strongly feminist show too, I think it's great that it doesn't ask people to choose sides between the magic of women of color and feminism.[clviii] Macy never forgets all that she is.

Muse of Memory: *Tray Barker, The very Last O.G.*: I don't know what made me look into this show on my Netflix queue. I don't know Morgan's comedy well, nor his work as an actor. Thank goodness I didn't let my own ignorance about his career keep me from viewing this series. I'm so glad that I saw this brilliant, funny, and beautifully written show.[clix] Morgan is extraordinary in it. It's the perfect vehicle for his talents. Without giving away anything more than the general description, Morgan's character, Tray Barker, is a former convict who goes back to his old neighborhood in Brooklyn to find it gentrified and many of the dynamics that he knew, including certain social codes, changed. Like many people in real life who return to the 'hood after being locked up, Barker has to figure out how to survive in a hurry. He relies on his particular Blerd skillset of making something out of nothing, in this case the fairly substandard institutional food he was given as an inmate into delicious cuisine. The sensitivity of the character in general is represented by his sensitivity in connecting things that don't seem to have much value separately.[clx] This unique ability protected him from rape and murder in prison and helped him to get a job on the outside. In addition to being a Blerd about low-nutrition cuisine, itself a formidable skill, Tray has the gold standard of self-taught knowledge: common sense/street smarts. Often when we talk about nerd/Blerd culture, we don't mention the many people in the neighborhood who tried to balance extreme underprivilege with community affirmation. Tray did it by becoming a drug dealer who got snitched out and did time. A story many of us know intimately in real life. He was, however, determined to make a way, applying his knowledge to his new environment. If he wasn't in such an extreme circumstance, he could've applied his natural and cultivated talents earlier in his life. Barker's story reminds me of a section of *The Autobiography of Malcolm X*, when Malcolm thinks about West Indian Archie's potential, given his extraordinary ability with numbers, if he'd had a chance to cultivate his mathematical gifts. One might also consider how great a lawyer Malcolm himself would've been had his White school teacher encouraged him rather than discouraged him. Malcolm found a way though, and I think about the substantial impact he made as an advocate for human rights, especially after his time in prison. Few trained lawyers could ever reach those heights of public impact. *The Last O.G.* is a dramedy, so Tray's trajectory is not presented in as heavy a fashion as Malcolm's autobiography, but the show has deep underlays and Morgan's subtle turns are riveting. In Tray's world, everyone's Black speech utterances are pointed, sharp, stark. 100% real talk. His former partner, Shannon, a.k.a. Shay (played by Tiffany Haddish[clxi]), tries to navigate the skills she needed to survive in the projects (fighting back unwaveringly) with the passive-aggressive whiter world she now inhabits. She also helps to convey those more unflinching assertive values to her new partner, who is a White male (Josh Birkeland, played by Ryan Gaul) and who takes his parenting responsibilities to their two Black children (also Tray's twins) seriously.[clxii]

Tray's understated comment about himself, that he gets along with everybody, speaks volumes about his skill in working between two worlds with what seems to be an insurmountable liability, being a Black man who was formerly incarcerated. Tray comes to terms with some of his earlier choices and reconciles with his very stern mother (played by beloved tv veteran Anna Maria Horsford) through the church. It is in the sanctity of the Black church that Tray confesses, says what he needs to say, and performs penitence as a profound speech act. His previously unresolved issues with his mother are reconciled by his honesty and through his children, her grandchildren. Josh's involvement is critical to this shift in the story. He feels his children should know their grandmother. It's a complex set of relationships that seems hopeful because, at their core, the principal characters deeply love the children above all else. Tray's literal "Come to Jesus" moment is a profound, community-based utterance that gives him another outlet for camaraderie that extends beyond his street life and prison life. This remarkable show continues to give us a sense of hope in this gritty world. Tray's ability to shapeshift in very different circumstances, while remaining true to his way of being, supported by Morgan's riveting sincerity, presents a hybridized concept of intelligence. This is an aspect of Blerd ability that cannot always be taught, as evidenced by sidekick/comic foil Bobby (played by Allen Maldonado), who never quite seems to "get it." It's as important as Tray's sincere interest in becoming a chef based on his *other* Blerd talent (cuisine).

Muse of Voicing, *Darling Nola*: Moving from culinary arts to visual arts, Nola Darling's new tv iteration by Spike Lee also has a Blerd focus as a formally trained painter. She was raised by two artistic Afrocentric parents and went to school for the visual arts (and has the college debts to prove it). In addition to being Blerdy about art, she has a talent for connecting to people, including "laying bare" the dynamics of human relationships openly and honestly. Like Tray Barker's character, this does not always mean that life is easy or that there aren't consequences for the array of choices she makes based on this ability. Both Tray and Nola are searching for freedom on their own terms despite society's efforts to label and confine them. Season two of *She's Gotta Have It* is especially noteworthy because the political implications of Nola's romantic, personal, and artistic relationships are heightened. Nola is angrier, more pointedly political, and more direct in dealing with the circumstances around her. In addition to this series being a very strong reference of its creator Spike Lee, it also incorporated the powerful presence of strong writers in his circle, including his siblings and long-time collaborators Joie Lee and Cinque Lee, multi-hyphenate phenom Eisa Davis, poet Lemon Andersen, producer/director Barry Michael Cooper, and playwrights Lynn Nottage and Antoinette Nwandu. Much can be said about each of these serious, accomplished writers who have spent years honing their crafts and applying them to Nola Darling. As a character, the extension of Nola's pathos, established through her complicated sex life/romantic life, into her total social speech act environment is sensible for a woman

who has lived and who continues to grow. Her character keeps finding and accepting herself and those she cares about irrespective of their relationship status with her. Her relationship with the Papo character, another Black person who is more vulnerable because he has another way of being in the world and has also been incarcerated, is noteworthy.

Like Macy in *Charmed*, Nola goes deeper into her own cultural roots for spiritual answers, and in Nola's case, solace.[clxiii] At the end of season two, the episode "I Am Your Mirror" heightens the politics of Nola's he*art*. Her conversation with one of her besties, 'Mekka, is the speech act version of threads that make up the art behind the curtain, weaved into/ as Nola's hair. It is a conversation about art representation vs. artistic process, another way of framing doing vs. describing to bring things full circle with Austin's premises here.[clxiv]

In this chapter I've written something slightly different than what I intended in the first iteration of this book. My early thoughts on Blerd culture were circumscribed by common parlance around nerd culture but with Black people: interests in speculative and science fiction, reading a lot, social awkwardness, etc. This was, in part, due to some social marginalization I'd experienced from my own community for being "bookish." In this second iteration, I want to keep to my conventional Blerd roots but also expand the idea of Blerdom to be more inclusive of people in our communities rather than to create another way for us to formulate separateness. Nerdom has changed across the board as information has become the coin of the realm, more valuable than the jock's athleticism and the suave guy's charm may have been in the past.

In the context of Blerdom, I'm going back to my 70s child-training of finding ways for us to connect with each other more as community members rather than find subcategories that allow us to indulge in a self-atomization that will ultimately destroy us. We stand together or fall separately, and that includes traditional Blerds with others not seen in the Blerd context before, but who are Blerds to their core. This goes both ways, of course. Those in the community who have mastered "these streets out here" should also be supporting those of us who go the more scholarly, readerly route and vice versa. Not looking for Eden here, that's not likely in any real community, but something closer to acceptance for our range of perspectives and ways of being. This'll be even more necessary as our communities are threatened with gentrification that disconnects us all from each other, making us easier pickings, as we see in discrete examples of racial violence, especially when we are alone.

Whether through digital means or, preferably, real time get-togethers, we have to keep working on being accepting of each other in our range of talents, abilities, and commitment to learning more and more about what we love.

Postscript:
What if you aren't "Black Like Me"?[clxv]

Love is hard work.[clxvi]—Miguel Algarín

"Shine your light for the world to see…":[clxvii] This part of the book proved more of a challenge to write because I'm not a huge fan of binaries. Things are often less clear to delineate than we think. And yet, we have long existed in a world, even right now, where binaries are resurrected before our eyes, separating us from each other, emphasizing the separations that continue to exist.

In much of this book I have used my thinking on Austin's ideas to generate a praise song riff, an aspect of empowerment for Black folks, and a reference point for the dispossessed and those who love us, who care. With my roots in a particular community, as a global citizen, in a specific place and time, I don't presume to write outside of my own experience. While I am averse to either/or frameworks,[clxviii] I am pragmatic about our real world at "this point in time."[clxix] In this postscript I'm addressing the challenges for those of good will who may find themselves to be in a "racially" privileged position or who simply are not Black. This postscript completes the book because we do live in a connected world where we intersect with others. If this book gets discussed outside of its perceived "core" audience, hopefully in a helpful way, it's because I believe there is a philosophical fluidity, using Austin's model as a lens, to analyze speech act environments beyond a specific bandwidth. I'm inspired by his writing to attempt it. We are all on this Earth together. As I said in the acknowledgments in another book, I

111

believe in the concept of universal love and care, even when considering hard aspects of our world, its hard center, its hard edges.

***

The performativity and subjectivity of race doesn't make race any less real. Although a construct, it has tangible implications for everyone (even if/as the definitions shift). One can be, unlike Austin's example of the cat on the mat,[clxx] both Black and non-Black.[clxxi] There are also many ways to be non-Black. Some Brits have adopted BAME as an amalgamation of Black, Asian, and Minority Ethnic to talk about a range of non-White ethnicities and races that include Black people in this mix. They're connected. Here in the States we could maybe say BLAIME (Black, Latinx, Asian, Indigenous/Indian, and Minority Ethnic (and/or, presumably, Middle Eastern). The concept of Blackness engages a spectrum that incorporates Blackness into it. (Blackness sometimes incorporates this spectrum into itself too: For example, BAME is a fairly recent acronym in the U.K. When I began traveling there twenty-five years ago, "Black" was a term that incorporated a range of people of color, the aggregate percentage of whom was/is tiny compared to the general U.K. population.) We could do a thought experiment on cheap headlines that would use the word "Blaime" regarding "us" because the spectrums within this group are often "blamed" for every aspect of societal dysfunction as a form of white supremacist doctrine (and we would probably "flip dat" through language within five seconds). While not Black, other people of color suffer racial hostility because they are not White (even as the definitions of White shift too[clxxii]).

One can also be Black and non-Black constatively (have non-African ancestry) yet be part of a Black cultural "adoption." The difference between this and appropriation, as an example, is the perlocutionary way the person and their utterances are *received by* the Black community (Black communities) rather than what the "performer" "gives off." For example, the "honorary" Black status afforded Bruce Lee and, say, Teena Marie.[clxxiii] (Black folks definitely wailed after her recent death as she was seen as "one of us.") Then there are the fearless political rebels like White abolitionist John Brown, so beloved by the Black community that his name and likeness entered into many Black songs and games. (I didn't realize the John Brown I heard about in play songs as a child was referring to a White historical figure until my teen years.) Contrast this love to people perceived as outright appropriators, such as Elvis Presley in the 1950s and 1960s, Vanilla Ice in the 1990s, and later, Justin Timberlake.[clxxiv] If we hold the idea of Black and non-Black together in our heads for a moment, one way of being non-Black is to be a person of color from another racial background.[clxxv]

There are ways of being *not* Black. One way is to be White (irrespective of cultural background because of binary social constructions). Another way would be through the metaphorical absence of Blackness— irrespective of the race of the performance utterer in contexts that are not Black—in which that Black person, or any other person, may be trying to fit. (In a way, I'm framing Austin's text in this last category and then reframing it *as* Black.) In other words, what is situated as a "racially neutral" environment (which often means a comfortably White environment).

Who do/does (what) with words is a query into "who's who" and "what's what." Who's in this "circle of life"? One of the pressing issues in the social media environment we cannot escape is the violence inherent in only speaking to people who agree with you already. (It's easier to telegraph violent thoughts against people not in your "group," especially within a group mentality.) We're witnessing weaponization through the limitation of speech environments. These tend to narrow definitions of meaning. Too often, we are not trying to figure things out together across lines. These limitations have the tendency to coarsen discussion by those who don't have to worry about the repercussions of inappropriate utterances in a socially uniform environment. It also makes one less accustomed to negotiating the different choices and variations in speech acts inherent in having conversations with diverse viewpoints. This ultimately renders the utterer less articulate. (I am aware that for marginalized, endangered/threatened communities, "circling the speech act wagons" feels safer, but we're never really safe and never really alone. That is part of our subjugation. We may as well be prepared for this scenario, even as we continue to affirm our specific group's beingness.)

The social necessity for personal growth and for overall social equality (through engagement with others) is being undermined by large scale exclusion and intimate exclusionary echo chambers. We must have the skill to converse with a range of perspectives, period. Not to be *liked*, per se, but to develop our abilities as social beings and to learn from, and appreciate, the consideration of new ideas.

For those with whom we vehemently disagree, being in diverse settings compels us to articulate our core values in an engaged way. It helps us to refine the distinction between what we mean and how it's perceived (locution and perlocution), even if it's just positive for ourselves.

Given the many social challenges we have by being in conversation with our curated circles of friends on social media, in fewer environments in the real and virtual world do we meet others who might share a different point of view. When these moments occur they can be in more personal social settings, such as one-on-one situations and smaller group situations.

In the cocktail party, artsy, elite circles, and in other places like one's employment environment, we are challenged to state things plainly. Sometimes plainspokenness is necessary to break up/expose embedded "understandings" of an environment. Other times that same outspokenness could immediately make the speech act "dismissible." Therefore subtle and diplomatic speech acts are necessary for the desired effect.

However, in these small circles problems of miscommunication and failed speech acts can also be derived from gaslighting.[clxxvi] Gaslighting[clxxvii] is the failsafe for ensuring pleasant conversation—aspects of behavitives (and specifically phatic acts—speech acts that emphasize social attitudes and feelings) of integrated interactions in racially integrated settings, and it must be identified through a speech act in some way. How one responds is often the question during an episode of gaslighting and I confess to not having a pat solution to this quandary. While this book goes out to a particular audience, this chapter speaks to the intersecting circles in which we often speak to each other.

Sometimes the person from a marginalized group in this situation doesn't want to be "Oprah on the couch" at the party, where people are compelled to share their racially uncomfortable moments with that person just because she is a Black woman who wrote something about race, for example (ahem). (*"Can a sista just get a cucumber sandwich? I mean…"*—I've had that thought myself more than once.) Here we are still the mirror of the dominant culture's gaze. On the other hand, I've had to encounter folks in the same hipster/chic/arty/douchey situation who feel so *comfortable* with me that they are self-prompted to say any stupid, racist, morally ambivalent thing that pops into their heads. They think it's because we're bonding at these settings but *really* it's because I'm outnumbered (outnumbered meaning one-on-one or any position of vulnerability due to power or numerical advantage). It's their world and I feel as if I'm seen as just the "entertainment," the intellectual/arty "help" in these so-called "sincere" situations.[clxxviii]

Another context that can emerge in these events: The assumption that the Black person (or person that's part of a politically marginalized group) is not smart enough or cosmopolitan enough to talk about anything other than their own designated race issue (or gender, sexuality, gender truth, "disability," class, age, etc.). This can be particularly frustrating for the Blerd who often has a deep knowledge and care for topics that they could be assumed to know by the majoritarian group *or maybe not most of them either.* Maybe they just got deeply into some topic whether it's expected or not.

***

Everyone thinks they're saying something different and "deep" in these awkward situations, something you've never heard before and a problem you (as other) need to solve for them right then and there so *they* can feel better as they move along the circuit (and to confirm to themselves that you are not a "problem"). It's a form of being "invited."[clxxix]

My eclectic knowledge base tends to be reassuring or *not* reassuring depending on the circumstance of presumptuousness I'm in: Either others find comfort in knowing that I know "White" things (Eurocentric things) or others can feel *dis*comfort that I know White things. It's almost as if people are surprised that I am well versed in the touchstones of the society that I have lived in *all my life,* much less that I might be able to appreciate, say, great art or philosophy, no matter who generates it.

***

The reality, however, is that we do have to deal with stuff sometimes and we have to deal with problematic stuff based on race while we're dealing with *other* stuff. We cannot avoid these interactions even if we are tempted to feel cynical about them. At obligatory work functions, at places where one thinks they can stick to what "we" have in common, as well as in venues where one is an artist, complex and sometimes unpleasant speech situations exist. As a racialized minority who's been on display and at the disposal of others since 1619 (in the U.S.), we have cultivated many ways of negotiating these and other speech environments. If we haven't, we may have sought someone to advise us on these social interactions. Depending upon the mentor, this person could be part of our group or someone who empathizes with the speaker and truly wants to help.

If one is lucky enough to have this type of support, one can master yet another speech act environment, and doing so is crucial for personal survival and sometimes even the thriving of our communities in pragmatic ways (for example to build personal relationships, to collaborate on community-based projects, to be able to do one's job effectively, to learn new things in order to share our knowledge *with* our communities, etc.).

 Even if one is a revolutionary and wants to "tear it all down," one has to know what's up. I've heard this generic "tear it down" and its variations, "let's shake things up" or "let's just do something different," suggestion more than a few times in the last few years but frequently not from those who truly mean it, or if they do, don't truly understand the implications of what these statements may mean.[clxxx] Those who do, however, know that they must be well-versed in the subtle transfer of information through speech acts between themselves and those they seek to liberate themselves from. An excellent example of this deep sophistication is the series of talks and debates Malcolm X had in elite

White circles, including with students at Oxford.[clxxxi] He was a master of wit and making it plain at the same time in these presentations. He was also deeply committed to grassroots organizing, which he did for the rest of his adult life, after he was freed from prison.

Using a differently effective approach to speech performance, organizing, and a precise attention to the nuances of the speaking (and singing) voice (as well as a sharp understanding of the fairly new medium of television), the great Fannie Lou Hamer's presentation during the Democratic National Convention in 1964 was such an extraordinarily effective speech act in the total speech environment that it frightened then-President Lyndon Johnson. He created an impromptu press conference *during her speech* to take the tv cameras off her commentary during the convention. She was also incredibly effective in the use of her singing voice as a tool for social change (in fact, Malcolm X once introduced her as an activist and singer at an event in Harlem on December 20, 1964[clxxxii]) for similarly political speech acts. Many extraordinary Black orators of the civil rights era, as well as times before and after, use the context of song to convey political commentary in speech acts: In addition to Hamer, Paul Robeson, Mahalia Jackson, Sweet Honey in the Rock, Billie Holiday, Marvin Gaye, Stevie Wonder, Prince, Martin Luther King Jr., Aretha Franklin, The Fisk Jubilee Singers, and Ella Baker,[clxxxiii] among others. It's important to note this fact here because the concept of "entertainment" as a forum for being "safe" in majoritarian environments is not always what it seems because these speech act environments are redefined by people who feel vulnerable in them. It's a tightrope act that people have figured out how to master in overt and covert ways.

If one isn't in such an either/or situation (blanket endorsement or tear it all down), in other words a more fluid context for speech acts, then mastering an array of speech environments and working with a diverse range of viewpoints is critical.

***

I have found intimate situations more vexing in this regard than larger, overtly politically charged ones or larger gatherings period. It could be because I'm a performer and have spoken publicly in various contexts for larger audiences for decades. In intimate speech acts, the speaker identified as being from a marginalized community must develop certain skills for these contexts that may take years to obtain. But what if you're part of the privileged group in an intimate setting? What do you say and how do you know if you are *unintentionally* part of the problem?[clxxxiv] Now that I've referenced specific speech environments for the other, time to turn to those who are not "othered" in this situation.

Black in a non-Black speech context at the same time can feel theoretical, conceptual. One who is in the privileged space/position can ask questions to themselves, questions they may not have considered in these intimate settings. In dealing with a Black/White dynamic or its variations, one from the privileged group can ask themselves several questions: What is "not Black" about me? When do I consider an encounter "Black enough" in this speech environment, and am I motivated to be in this encounter/affirm this encounter primarily so I can say "I spoke with a Black person and learned something and now *I* feel 'better'"? The not-Black person might feel empowered/emboldened enough to feel they're a bit "Black" themselves, as part of the desire to be *cool*. (Oy. The *worst*.[clxxxv])

***

Why choose the cocktail setting, intimate hangout, as a location of radicalized performance? In my mind, these low-key, seemingly friendly social settings reveal much about what people feel they do and don't have permission to say, where they feel comfortable. Cocktail parties imply an elite air that urges pretension, status, civility, and a false sense of ease. They are great situations in which to reflect upon Erving Goffman's ideas about "the front."[clxxxvi] There are other, more charged situations in which the stakes are higher and more apparent. I do think, however, that there are more clear guidelines on how to act, how to be, in difficult situations that often require mediation (workplace harassment, civil rights marches, trials, etc.).[clxxxvii]

***

In the *Autobiography of Malcolm X,* toward the end of the book, Alex Haley reports that the legendary human rights leader was asked by an earnest young White woman "what she could do" about race problems in America. Brother Malcolm said "nothing." He was a great artist of "The Dozens" throughout his life and that was definitely an "ooh snap" moment. In the autobiography, Malcolm X later regretted that quip and said that what she, and others, can do is go back to their own communities, their families, neighbors, and friends and talk about issues of racism and bigotry that they have been exposed to, and may in fact embody, towards working to put a stop to these problems where *they* are. In other words, to positively "do things" with words and other actions among their own social circles to effect change.

***

Oftentimes, it's just left to us. Those who are subject to racist bullying, torture, and harassment are expected to solve the problem of their own oppression. We usually do it ourselves. That "problem" can take various forms: From addressing and solving systemic racism to being forced to make people who are uncomfortable with your race "feel better" (—

without being too self-reflexive. It's usually not framed this way, but that's often what it is).

We end up in the odd position of "putting a mirror up to [someone's] nature."[clxxxviii] People want to see reflections of themselves in a way that makes them happy. That's an aspect of *all* human nature I think. What I'm considering here is at whose expense this reflection occurs. If this sense of being "reassured" becomes more important than coming up with solutions and environments where *all people feel safe* from racist (sexist, transphobic, etc.) danger and can be themselves on their own terms, it should be considered in this way, and changed if possible. The more vulnerable person in this situation also wants to not have to explain themselves to others in order to be a vehicle for the majoritarian person to presume their own self-congratulatory "self-isolation" (e.g.: "I'm not like the rest of the people here who are like me").

There is a third issue with this cocktail party/intimate scenario for those subject to this kind of small-scale "warfare" provocation, and it has to do with dimensionality, or as my inner Blerd feels compelled to say: "Space: the final frontier."

The final voyage in these intimate settings, whether romantically intimate, collegially intimate, or just logistically or numerically small, is the permission by those in a privileged position to simply take up more space (literally and metaphorically). In the locutionary section of Austin's thoughts, he talks about illocution as what one means/intends (while perlocution is how it's perceived).

Illocutionarily, the questions by those of privilege to those who are not but may be in a similar social setting, is to question so that they may *control the discourse*. Sometimes this means within the conversation itself, but often it means to use the conversation as "field research" to hold forth as an authority *instead of* the aggrieved party. It is to take up space and dominate social settings even as an outsider to the aggrieving situation, because one has the power to do so by dominating the space. If this is the case, how then can one use one's privilege effectively without oppression of the subjugated?

***

One of my favorite popular culture examples of this breaking down of illocutionary and perlocutionary protocols in social settings that is not based on minoritarian status is the wonderful made-for-tv British film *The Girl in the Cafe.*[clxxxix] In it, the lead female protagonist, Gina, portrayed by Kelly Macdonald, disrupts a fancy event to question the assumptions and smug behavior of the guests who are supposedly doing "good." While the reviews of the film were mixed (some of the reviewers seemed downright defensive as if they were guests at the fictional dinner party themselves), the interest I have in the film stems from the many scenes in which Gina "gives" (conveys through her pointed comments) something that is antithetical to what she "gives off" (her visual impression). I'm using Goffman's language here to dovetail with Austin's ideas about the meaning of words being subject to the performance event. While there are situations that would or would not encourage fairness, equality, and care because they are disruptive, Gina also uses her beauty, her well-dressed status, and her *seeming* belonging (in other words she passes as someone who is invested in the power of that class[cxc]) to speak truth to power. The film does not put the responsibility on those who are the direct victims of the misery she describes to solve the problem or even to articulate it. They don't have access to this event. (In this case, poor African people/nations in debt to the West.) She takes it upon herself to do the heavy lifting, not in a self-congratulatory way and certainly not to affirm a desire for power. She does it because she is the only person who is willing to in that intimate setting at that moment.[cxci]

The onus often falls on the marginalized themselves (or the less marginalized among the marginalized) to bring these issues to light even when outnumbered and the most vulnerable. A non-fictional/artistic example of someone utilizing privilege to explore/expose issues of class (and race is certainly implied) is Jamie Johnson, whose influential independent documentary film, *Born Rich*, literally put a critical lens to the intimate speech acts between the younger members (and a few parents) of the socialites of the American upper-wealthy-class.

Often those of us who get "guest status" into variations of these echelons are expected to be exceptional and typically representative of the marginalized and to perform both these roles all the time. In other words, to be whatever role makes people feel most comfortable and yet, elevated, to continue to allow *them* to take up most of the space in their privilege.

The shorthand way of considering these problems, when one is not a Black person or anyone else not in a privileged position under the specific circumstances, is to ask questions like: How much space am I taking up and at whose expense? Is the purpose of this speech act I'm giving to illuminate/help/support/solve a problem or to just make *me* feel comfortable? Is the person I'm asking questions to empowered by our conversation or are they simply, for me, a mirror amplifying my reflected glow? Or more simply: Do I consider this person my equal as a human being in every way?

Two artists come to mind as I'm writing this who have exemplified these existential questions by their own means: One is the pop singer Crystal Waters in her classic House music hit "Gypsy Woman (She's

Homeless.)"[cxcii] In this song, Waters wrote lyrics about a homeless woman who's "just like you and me," who wears makeup to beg for money, disrupting the assumption that all homeless women are unkempt. (The song was inspired by a real woman Waters encountered who lost her middle-class job and became homeless.) Another example is the visual and performance artist Michael Bramwell.[cxciii] In Bramwell's case, he utilizes the assumption that he, as a Black man, would be perceived as being in a subservient position in art world contexts as well as in neglected areas of Black communities. He upends this notion of his Black male "performance" in these contexts, as well as at sites of mass trauma such as Hiroshima, Japan, and Goree Island, Senegal. He wears a worker's uniform identified with manual labor and cleaning services, and uses a broom to thoroughly swipe these spaces. He attempts to literally sweep them "clean." He thereby brings attention to the literal and metaphorical unclean sources of these sites.

In a way, these artists mirror each other (as well as Macdonald's character Gina and Johnson as a filmmaker), but all engage with various strata of privilege to bring to light a story or condition that would otherwise go unrecognized. While Waters and Bramwell are Black, they are of a different class status (as well-paid artists) than the people they are performing for/as in their speech acts. Many of the "Occupy" youth and not-youth were bringing attention to people not of their class or other forms of privilege, to the locations of people who are privileged. They utilize their "exceptionalism."[cxciv]

These examples, both Black and non-Black, emphasize the subjectivity of what we consider constative. What we consider factually descriptive aspects of a person: their race, gender, gender presentation, class, embodiment, neurodiversity,[cxcv] sexuality, ethnicity, etc., are subject to redefinition, as is one's alliances to those groups and to oppressive power.

These definitions and redefinitions are all performative even when they *seem* constative.

***

None of these ideas are new. We have always had the tools to negotiate and renegotiate with power towards a more just world in our everyday lives and through extraordinary non-Black heightened language (like Shakespeare's and Tolkien's) as well as other forms of performance. *None of these presented speech acts are neutral and their locution,*[cxcvi] *their fundamental meaning as utterances, and their references to power, can be changed.* What, at the heart of things, do those who perform these roles intend? (In both public and intimate speech acts, what these acts do and how they are received can tell us what is actually being performed through language.) Austin may or may not have intended for his work to be used this way, but through his open-source, open-hearted, open-*purpose*[cxcvii] work, and through the long-held expertise of Black *(re-)creation of* language, its elements, and its purpose, there are road maps to knowing, to change: to the love, care, and equality of all throughout this Earth.

Coda: Morenita of the World

Although this book has mainly presented thoughts on philosophy applied to a particular perspective on one African American life, for the past year I've traveled a lot overseas and it reminded me, in this second edition, of how America-focused many accounts or comments by American authors are, of whatever demographic background. Most other folks in the world see themselves as more of an international community than we do. This is represented in, for example, the idea that one is *supposed to be multilingual*, that this is an asset and part of one being knowledgeable of the world.

The first time I went overseas was to Brazil as a college student. As soon as I deplaned and moved through security (this was way before 9/11/2001 so it was a quicker and more chaotic process), the Brazilian security guy I encountered as I was getting my bag had all sorts of comments about American politics. He spoke very little English but made it clear that he had an opinion about the U.S. President at the time. I was shocked and embarrassed because I didn't have any opinion about the President of Brazil at that point. My first encounter with this security guy made me really reflect on my privileged lack of knowledge.

I still don't know as much as I should, and of course with the pervasiveness of the internet one could find out who the President of any country is, as well as know much of its politics in moments.

What the internet *can't* necessarily give you, however, is a sense of what it means to really be part of the world, to feel connected as a member of a global community in real life, in fact, as a *being* on this planet. Sometimes, in fact, the passive *observation* of the world can make one feel *less connected* to the world.

The implications of the disconnection are vast. It undermines our empathy and lowers the stakes in our minds and hearts.

I made a decision in 2016[cxcviii] to get off social media. Mainly because it was an election year and I knew, as a political junkie, I'd be overloaded, but also because I found that it was getting in the way of me being in the world and it was eating into my writing/creative time as well as my pedagogical and organizational work. I also avoid carrying electronic instruments unless I need them where I'm going.

These two decisions have radically changed the quality of my life. Firstly, I find that I am more in the world *and* of it.[cxcix] I'm less consumed by clickbait and propaganda and my mood is better. I feel that I can manage things.

I notice things: flowers, children, trees, birds, neighbors. A sense of stress "out there" is palpable, and the overwhelmedness of others is nearly universal. I was feeling myself shutting down being so plugged in, and now I'm more (selectively) in tune with others.

Dispassionate, lack of empathy leads to the destruction of the self, what makes us caring beings. It hurts. Shutting down is an understandable reaction. Rather than taking this course, though, we can do something else: Build communities in real time with real people.

Detaching from electronics forces me to be more considerate, to show up on time because I can't send that text saying that I'm on my way five minutes after the appointed time. The world feels more vibrant, alive. I get out of my own head more. Besides the naval gazing and blithe observations of which getting off electronics has made me aware, freedom from constant interneting has also placed me more in the world and has focused me on a few important things rather than many distracting things.

As an American Black woman, I feel justified focusing on my identity, but that does not absolve me of not caring about others who aren't like me, or the planet itself. We must notice others. Many of our human rights/civil rights heroes did this: They saw our struggles and our victories in the movements and vulnerabilities of others. They observed the humanity of others (and the importance of this biosphere we all exist in).

Their empathy is a practice in applied love and universal care, and they did not have to sacrifice their caring about their own communities to care about others. In fact, their concerns about their own communities and identities were based in these connections. The great writer and thinker who recently passed on, Toni Morrison, discusses empathy extensively in her work.

What I'm finding is that I can do one or two small things. I can notice a few things and focus on those. (We Blerds/nerds have really learned how to focus on something a lot, part of the training…) It might be something radically universal (like climate change, national LGBTQ legislation, immigration reform) and something very local (reparative art therapy for a vulnerable population, get out the vote campaigns, letter writing, meeting with a particular small group that needs help in your local community).

The use of ordinary language as action brings different types of people together. Ordinary language is not exclusionary. It can be, and has often been, applied to political action uttered to affirm oneself as a person in this whole world in the particulars and in the aggregate. When Austin talks about words having meaning, a certain intent, and a certain effect, he's talking about a range of speech acts, including duplicitous political speech, and he can also be talking about meaningful individual efforts through ordinary language every day.

His theory leads us to think about something else too: Can we exist in this world and be our best, most productive, ambitious, and happy selves, and it not be at the expense of others but in tandem with the world? Is it possible?

This is *the* fundamental question of the day, of humankind. I think the answer is yes but it will be hard work, as love is. We have to ask the question and assume that this is the fundamental value we all share. I look to my recently departed friend Steve Cannon and his legacy in this regard. Although he focused on the arts, he created an environment at his home/workspace/studio/salon/publishing company/workshop "A Gathering of the Tribes" that epitomized the concept of benefitting, but not at the expense of others, through sharing. Although quite erudite, Steve spoke in ordinary language, was an exceptional listener, and was genuinely interested and attentive in his conversations. As I mentioned in a small homage to Steve that I wrote recently, even people who didn't get along with each other got along with Steve. He *sweetly insisted on it.* It's a rare skill and one that requires the present, human touch.

Technology has enriched us so much that we don't need to do many things that we used to have to do in order to survive.ᶜᶜ We don't need to use as much land to produce food. We don't need to work people as hard to build a society. We can have a more efficient, easier time of it.

But what about motivation?, some say. Will people be motivated to work hard if things are "too easy"? My counter question is: "Can the motivation be to make the world a better place?" To see how brilliant we can be and how caring, using technology in moral thoughtful ways? Can we build a society in real life, as well as through tech, that benefits everyone?[cci] How invested can we be in the concept of Love—how ambitious can this make us? These motivations are what lead people to fight for freedom, to create new technologies that help others, to serve and uplift "the least among us."

Talk is a form of action and there are actions that are forms of utterance. The law that Austin regularly references, the "promise" that Shoshana Felman wittily takes from Austin's theory, the gendered subjectivity of language and performance that Judith Butler illuminates, the complexity of saying something again and it meaning something different that Derrida illuminates—all these philosophers use words to uncover the deep meaning of humankind that frames/reframes the art of language.[ccii]

Here we are: at a crossroads of what we will do with words, meaning what we will do with our actions. What will we invoke? What manifestation of our world will we speak into being? What do we want to be present for? What do we do? What do we make? What *do*, we have to *say*, for *ourselves*?

Our world depends on our understanding of ourselves and our understanding of it. The title of this book is a question that leads to a question: Who (does) do what with words? What do we do? What will we choose to do, together? I will be investigating these ideas further in the other two books in this trilogy of considerations of Austin's theory and how it can be applied now.

After/Word, Black and Blerd

by Robin D.G. Kelley

J. L. Austin delivered the lectures that became *How to Do Things with Words* at Harvard University in 1955. I wonder how long he stayed in Cambridge and whether he wandered off campus? I could imagine him arriving that summer, traveling to the Berkshires and catching a lecture by Langston Hughes on jazz and blues at the Music Inn. Or perhaps perusing the shelves at Harvard's bookstore and discovering the newly published *The Sweet Fly Paper of Life*, Roy DeCarava's Harlem photographs with text by Hughes. Scanning the stunning, earthy photos of black people, his wandering eyes would have settled on the words of Hughes's fictional narrator, Sister Mary Bradley. He surely would have recognized his theory of language. Speaking of her son-in-law, Sister Mary muses, "This world is like a crossword puzzle in the Daily News— some folks make the puzzles, others try to solve them. But Jerry don't worry about no puzzles a-tall. Worriation ain't no part of his nature." Hughes' everyday speech ventriloquized through the stout and clever Sister Mary doesn't just describe Jerry; it drops some knowledge about how the world works and our place in it.

If Austin had picked up a black newspaper, he may have come across Zora Neale Hurston denouncing the U.S. Supreme Court decision on Brown v. Board of Education, which she felt insulted black people's intelligence by presuming that all Negroes preferred to go to school with white kids. For this Hurston was skewered by the leading black intelligentsia and political class. Journalist Roi Ottley called her a "handkerchief head" Negro, and took her to task for writing, "We talk about the race problem a great deal, but go on living and laughing and striving like everybody else." Austin would have immediately recognized her illocutionary act and the perlocutionary effect on her erstwhile critic. And he undoubtedly would have marveled at her phatic expression of the power of behabitives to combat words or gestures intended to belittle, degrade, and subjugate a people. Black folks know words do the work of keeping us whole, living our lives not without laughter, surviving and striving.

Had Austin stepped just a little beyond the boundary of Harvard yard, who knows, he may have encountered the words of these two OB's (Original Blerds), allowing him to access another world of speech acts that would have confirmed and deepened his basic thesis. I suspect the result may have produced something akin to the spirit animating Tracie Morris's breathtaking *Who Do With Words: A Blerd Love Tone Manifesto.* Having read her doctoral dissertation and the first iteration of *Who Do*, dancing through/with/to what amounts to an eighteen-chapter manifesto evoked an image of Hughes and Hurston meeting Austin at Junior's Restaurant and Bakery in Brooklyn, performative utterances flying back and forth over cheesecake and coffee.

But that's just the feeling, the sensibility I got from the book. All analogies aside, Who Do With Words is the voice of Tracie Morris, uncut, raw, embodied, hilarious, solemn, resolute, whispered to a shout, words that do shit. As manifestos go, this one is playful, cunning, angular like Monk, free like Cecil, fierce like Grace, sexy-smart- shapeshifting like Prince. Words tumble promiscuously but cut with the precision of an exacto knife. But what we have here is much more than a manifesto. It is autobiography, moving memory and experience and being through epochs of Black Power, Hip Hop's flowering, and Afro-futures, through the virtual realms of dungeons and dragons, through the Blerd world of groundation and boundless imagination. It is a work of theory, advancing Austin's thesis by situating Black speech acts in a political context, which means collapsing the space between everyday speech and the poem. She digs deep into Black creative speech and performance, both in the ways these are used within the culture and the way they have been appropriated by the white mainstream as a means of reinventing themselves and disappearing the rest of us. These infelicitous encounters are never permanent since our arsenal of words is infinite, and we have a way of "living and laughing and striving like everybody else" do. Most importantly, Morris sets out to deploy "Austin's philosophy as a lens for Black freedom" but in so doing, turns to Black expressions of freedom as a lens to interrogate, repurpose, and queer Austin's philosophy.   That, dear reader, is Blerd World Liberation!

Who do better to bring on the revolution than Tracie Morris? Way, way before she encountered the bespectacled pipe-smoking British philosopher, she understood the power of words—that words do things. She is widely recognized as one of the most innovative and consequential performance poets of the last half century. A visionary, a medium, a storyteller possessed of extraordinary perlocutionary powers, capable of locating and seizing upon a listener's every exposed nerve ending, Tracie Morris is a word magician who can make virtually every utterance into music and manifesto. Face it, all of her manifestos are love tones, for this is how she speaks, what she stands for, what she embodies whether on a stage or in a classroom or a cypher or chatting on the subway. Everyday speech and the poem are collapsed, along with the unconscious, dreams of freedom, the will to exist. Who Do With Words simply gives us an even more powerful map to the sunlit, non-binding and non-binary world Blerds have been seeking for centuries.

Acknowledgements

Thanks to all my fam (here and otherwhere) and sibling John and my mom, an Afrocentric art Blerd. Special shout out to the *Black Geeks Nerds of Color* posse founded by Jermaine Hall in 2016, and its predecessor, for me, the *Dive-In Movies* crew, founded by David Barclay Moore in 2012. The Blerd posse is strong!

Big thanks to Fred M. and many of my Blerd and non-Blerd nerds, especially those academics who, despite academy politics, teaching loads, families, and other obligations manage to write right (a lot) like: Charles Bernstein, Samuel R. Delany, Sarah Schulman, Amiri Baraka and Sonia Sanchez. Y'all show me how it's done. How to make it work in a *practical* way. Thanks to the many recording and theater artists I know who stay *on that grind* putting out the work and who inspire me to get over myself, my fears, and just continue to *try* to make work that endures. It's never finished, it's always just starting again. The love is in the making and making the effort. Thanks also to Lisa Birman for suffering through my myriad of thoughts to copyedit this second edition and to Charles Alexander, the patience of Job publisher of this volume who has put up with all my last-minute changes in this rippling, big bouncy baby toddler of a book. The mistakes are literally mine, specially those both Lisa and Charles A. tried to correct! I'm super-grateful to Dr. Robin D.G. Kelley who was gracious enough to write an afterward-after/word for this edition. He also served on my dissertation defense committee — and he was tough too! He also encouraged me to apply to NYU's Performance Studies doctoral program back in the day. And the rest, as they say… well, the rest is this book, actually.

I am deeply indebted to the great philosophical genius John Langshaw Austin, whose legacy looms large and to whom I bow in this first effort in my triptych of writings into his work. (This is the "heart" part. The "mind" part, *How We Do (Other) Things with Words,* is forthcoming, I hope, soon. I'm still working out the philosophical "spirit" book of the final part of the triptych. Stay tuned.) I'm deeply appreciative to the British Library in London for keeping Mr. Austin's recordings well- preserved and available to the public.

I'm so happy for all the nerds/dorks/Blererds and geeks of all stripes who have been fellow travelers. Your presence always makes me feel as if I'm in good company. Those who love to learn are never truly alone.

I'm grateful to my students, especially those in my Speech Act Theory classes, and similar classes, , who are now becoming too numerous to list. After finishing my dissertation on Austin a dozen years ago, it's been great talking through Austin's luminous ideas with my students.

I also want to thank the wonderful administrator Noel Rodriguez, Administrative and Academic Services Director at NYU's Performance Studies program, who quietly, rigorously, and unassumingly has made it possible for many of us to get over the intimidating hurdles that made it possible for us to get PhDs in Performance Studies, and therefore was instrumental to me writing this book based on my dissertation ideas. Noel is one of the most elegant academic systems Lerds (Latinx nerds). My highest praise.

I'm very grateful to my teachers in all my undergrad and grad programs, including the colleagues who unerringly and staunchly support me. I"m also grateful to my family immediate and extended, including a couple I've mentioned here, for supporting me with their pride of/for me and everyday speech acts of care and kindness. I"m grateful to my "ride or die" dear friends who continue to stand with me on this adventurous, less-traveled road.

I am humbled beyond words and thankful beyond measure to all of J.L. Austin's students. I'm in your debt. They lovingly compiled his work and their notes to ensure Austin'shis brilliance is present in the world. I wouldn't be who I am if it weren't for your care. Thank you.

Endtones

i. The actor/director/producer/comic Aisha Tyler uses this phrase to great effect in her voicing of Lana in the animated series *Archer* (FXX).

ii. Or as Ta-Nehisi Coates acerbically notes, the phrase "Well, Actually…" in his response to Bob Costas' commentary after the death of Muhammad Ali in the article: "Bob Costas To Muhammad Ali—'Well Actually…'" *The Atlantic*, Jun 6, 2016. This is also a reference to the legendary retort of Sidney Morgenbesser to J.L. Austin's comments on unlikelihood of the double-positive meaning a negative during one of Austin''s speeches: "yeah yeah" a.k.a. "yeah, right." was Morgenbesser's retort. I'm using "Yeah but," to is split tting the difference in meanings here.here.

iii. Brooklyn foundation, U.S. southern roots, Pan-African, world citizen.

iv. *Poetry and the Fate of the Senses, by* Susan Stewart, University of Chicago Press, 2002.

v. This, I feel, is the fundamental horror of these "annoyance" calls to police officers of living/breathing/playing/swimming/driving/shopping/visiting/working while Black. It is raising the question of our right to exist anywhere in this country and, for that matter, on Earth.

vi. A claim that J.L. Austin makes at the beginning about his lectures in *How To Do Things with Words*.

vii. This is according to my mom, but I think this is a well-known trope.

viii. This is a riff on the ballad/standard "Spring Can Really Hang You Up the Most." Lyrics by Fran Landesman, music by Tommy Wolf, 1955.

ix. I know that makes the reading a bit more work and hopefully also a bit more playful.

x. To quote the Sly Stone song: "*I* am everyday people." I say (sing) this and I think Austin is saying this too.

xi. Or maybe this book is a "ride or die" side kick/side chick to *HTDT*. Someone is the protagonist for the "story" but that doesn't always mean that the ally isn't equally important to the "action."

xii. I'm so grateful that the last words I heard form Jose were encouraging ones about my work on Austin. More shout outs: Allen S. Weiss and Fred Moten also sat on my exam committee. Karen Shimikawa, Tavia Nyongo, Farah Griffith, and Robin D.G. Kelley sat on my dissertation committee. Thanks to you all for getting me through.

xiii. I don't mean this in the abstract. Kidnapped Africans enslaved in the United States were not thought to be humans but chattel, and therefore *objects* to be traded. As objects we were not considered worthy of *human* rights. This is beyond simply "bad treatment." We had a different status and were not considered to have souls or to suffer in the same way. This projection of non-humanness onto us put us in a distinct category legally, socially, and conceptually. The assumption that Black people feel pain less continues to affect empathy and medical treatment we receive to this very day: https://www.huffingtonpost.com/2014/03/04/children-think-black-people-feel-less-pain_n_4891296.html

xiv.   Here I am using performative African -American phrases to demonstrate my reference perspective in arguing with him.

xv.   I should've known this would be part of my life's work just *because I was so mad at him*. This was a rom-com level fit of pique on my part! Anybody's idea that evokes that level of passion always ends up "getting the girl," ahem.

xvi.   A famous "miscommunication" regarding names, baseball positions, and performances by the comedy duo Abbott and Costello. They debuted the routine circa 1936.

xvii.   A line from the *KJV Bible, Book of Numbers,* 23:23, and also the first line Samuel Morse telegraphed long distance in the U.S. in 1844. Here I mean any need to try to articulate the extraordinary, whether it's deified or not.

xviii.   As well as the more emphatically spoken and implied temptations in the red-light district in the film version of *The Wiz.*

xix.   a.k.a. AAVE's "He jus' *playin'.*"

xx.   In African American culture there has long been this notion of "marking" someone with words, as in the phrase "Don't *mark* me." Lots of room for Austinian applications in that phrase.

xxi.   From the poem and song of the same title, "Philosophy of the Cool" by Sekou Sundiata on recording *The Blue Oneness of Dreams,* Mouth Almighty Records, 1997. Here I'm lowercasing the "b" because I don't claim to know what Sekou intended with both uses of this homonym. I know that he definitely did mean the color black in at least one use here so I erred on the side of caution.

xxii.   Of course Cornelius Eady's important book *Brutal Imagination* comes to mind here.

xxiii.   A chapter title from Amiri Baraka's book *Blues People,* Morrow Quill Paperbacks, 1963.

xxiv.   My immediate family sees "the n-word" as a form of this thingification, objectification, dehumanization, and this is why we didn't use it in our house even if we secretly cussed every once in a while. That's not something that was generally said.

xxv.   Here I mean this in the Ellison "Invisible Man" sense.

xxvi.   The exempting of the speech acts of stagehands in *HTDT* is literally true and not a flourish on my part. I'm glad that Austin gave props to these unsung heroes of the stage, very humane of hime to do so, and it made me more frustrated that he didn't include the poets, writers and actors and others too.

xxvii.   In fact, I'd say this is what the difference is between a city dweller and a random gentrifier. You know you dwell with others here and that includes those on the inside and outside (with the dual urban implications of these terms). More on this in subsequent chapters.

xxviii.   Maybe it was in tandem with the "everyday sounds" of his teaching too: the squeaking chair, the discordant sounds of chalk on a board, his natural genuflections of stuttering. The normalcy of this giant's articulation in his natural environment. I wept at the "total speech environment." How precious these stolen moments are.

xxix.   I also read too many Harlequin romances as a kid. I'm way too corny with this kind of *touchy-feely* stuff, to riff off one of Jose's mentors, Eve K. Sedgwick's book *Touching, Feeling,* (Duke University Press, 2003), even though Sedgwick was definitely talking about things much more profound than bodice-ripper novels, the multi-sensory notion of touching and feeling, the connection between sense and sentiment, is worth noting. The voice is a channel for both and, therefore, the performative utterance is part of the voice"s channelling.

xxx.   Inspired by real-life tales from the 'hood as well as that *Sex and the City* episode (from another fantasy-laden interpretation of a cityscape) when Carrie got her Manolos stolen from her feet out in the street!

143

xxxi.   We do this remaking of words in joyful contexts too: The innovations of Black personal names during and after enslavement are examples of our linguistic innovations. By naming/renaming, we build our individual Edens. One person by one person, a garden, an aspiration, hope for a better world. One example of the resistive aspect of self-naming was described by Laurence Tureaud, a.k.a. "Mr. T," renowned for the *Rocky* movies and the 1980s tv show *The A Team*. When asked in an interview why he legally changed his original name, he said: "I self-ordained myself Mr. T so the first word out of everybody's mouth is 'Mr.' That's a sign of respect that my father didn't get, that my brother didn't get, that my mother didn't get." Quoted from the blog FestivalReviews.org under the heading "Happy Birthday: Mr. T."

xxxii.   The actor/director and professor David Schwingle and I have had many great discussions on this legendary abolitionist figure.

xxxiii.   For instance, some people read Genesis and say humans have dominion over this world and we can do anything we want to it. Others read the same passages and say we are caretakers with the beings who share this home. The phrases in the Bible are descriptive but their force, what people think these words do and in turn what humans *can* do, is poetic and is certainly not neutral or purely descriptive.

xxxiv.   As exemplified in the Black expression "Don't put my name in your mouth" and/ or ""Take my name out your mouth." And the banality of evil in public policy and bureaucracy that can save or destroy lives with the stroke of a pen.

xxxv. Line from my poem "Fred Rogers," 2003. This poem was in honor of the person and persona "Mr. Rogers" and how his unapologetic "corniness" and quintessential goodness were a moral guidepost in the flashy context of other kid shows. Maybe he was one of my pre-precursors to appreciating Austin's "corniness."

xxxvi. "What I shall have to say here is neither difficult nor contentious; the only merit I should like to claim for it is that of being true, at least in parts." First line of *How To Do Things with Words*, J. L. Austin, 1962.

xxxvii. This line was one of the ones that got my hackles up at first: "Surely the words must be spoken 'seriously' and so as to be taken 'seriously'? … I must not be joking, for example, nor writing a poem." *HTDT*, 9.

xxxviii.   The absence of Black presence as a pointed political statement is something I explored in a previous book. In *handholding: 5 kinds* (Kore Press, 2016), I approach Stanley Kubrick's film *Eyes Wide Shut* as a political commentary on race, gender, and sexuality through the *absence* of diversity in the film. I've been wrestling with this idea for a few years now and wondered if there was a possibility that Austin was making a similar point that I felt Kubrick was making in this regard. I don't see it in Austin, but that doesn't mean the idea can't be considered using Austin's theories, whether he intended this use or not.

xxxix. "…a performative utterance will, for example, be in a peculiar way hollow or void if said on the stage, or void if said by an actor on the stage, or if introduced in a poem, or spoken in soliloquy…Language in such circumstances is in special ways—intelligibly—used not seriously, but in ways parasitic upon its normal use—ways which fall under the doctrine of the etiolations of language." *HTDT*, p. 22.

xl.   Line from the chorus of the song "Juicy" by Notorious B.I.G., Arista Records, 1994.

xli.   Referencing the song "Talkin' Loud and Sayin' Nothing," James Brown and Bobby Byrd, Polydor Records, 1970. I think he could also be alluding to the Black expression "cuttin' up" here.

xlii.   This is my retort to Eddie Murphy's lampooning of James Brown (for instance, in the hot tub skit during his *Saturday Night Live* stint). Many years ago I gave a talk on this.

xliii.   In *The Presentation of Self In Everyday Life* (Anchor Books, 1959), sociologist Erving Goffman discusses "the front" extensively, and in a sense his description is complimentary to this African American expression.

xliv.   Especially when the racist is caught. The recent spate of nomenclatures for racist White people caught on camera and, subsequently, fired from their jobs due to their toxic proximity to company branding almost always has them saying that they aren't racist, even when saying clearly racist things and doing racist things that aren't worded (stereotyping, blackface, etc.).

xlv.   In Austin's framing, speech acts are "void" when their utterances are logically impossible, contradictory, or mutually exclusive to the intention of the expression.

xlvi.   The Black Queer snap: "No shade, but shade" works particularly well in this context. As many marginalized people know, the level of sophistication we need to survive is often through the nuanced rooms in the language houses we build.

xlvii.   I don't know when I first heard this compound word, definitely from my mom, but I'm trying to bring it back into parlance. It's just too mellifluous to resist. It also qualifies a qualifier, thereby reinforcing the double-negative linguistic rules that are often standards of Ebonic/AAVE speech.

xlviii.   Particularly when this behavior takes the form of gaslighting. More on this later.

xlix.   Clarification of grammatical rules regarding "racial" terms: I capitalize White, Black, etc. because it has been long established that these terms are not literally adjectival regarding the color of the person's skin, but a reference to their American "ethnicity" (even if it might be a composite of other ethnicities). I do not capitalize the term "white supremacy" because the capitalization reinforces, performs as, the racist hierarchy inherent in the term (just as capitalization often does with place names, names of persons, official titles, etc.). In other words, I choose not to enable the racism or "supremacy" of the term by capitalizing "white" (or the term "supremacy," for that matter) *in this particular context*, but do outside of this phrase, as I do Black, Asian, Latinx, etc.

l.   For instance, that European classical music is just "better" rather than it being one form of music that one can like for its beauty, sophistication, etc., as one would like, say, Indian Classical music using tabla, the in-depth postmodernist wordplay of Jean Grae, or the high-concept traditional visual art of the original Australians. All of these are "classic," but one doesn't have to appreciate one at the expense of another or only call one "Classical." When one applies a so-called "neutral" term like this to only one group's type of music, then one is subtly, or not so subtly, saying that everything else that is traditional is inherently inferior, making superiority/supremacy a subtextual "given." Can one like Beethoven's music better than, say, City Girls? Sure. Just as one can say that Kendrick Lamar is more sonically complex than Kenny G. The work in the world is sometimes beautiful, sometimes complicated, and people do have cultural pride. It's when we assume that affirmation of ourselves, or groups we connect with, has to be at the expense of other groups or people of good will, that supremacist notions take hold, *especially when the larger structures support the oppression of other groups*. Subtextually or not, the concept of supremacy must be challenged at every opportunity. It must be interrogated, especially in language. Hopefully, we'll get to the point where we can appreciate the range of beauty and wonder in art, knowledge, and cultures without the need to enforce hierarchies on everything.

li.—And first cousin of the non-craptastic friend of Dr. Watson…

lii.   There's a great updated reference to this old saw in the Stanley Kubrick film *Eyes Wide Shut*, when Bill Harford's wife asks him how her hair looks. He says she looks beautiful but she notes that he didn't look at her. He says that she always looks beautiful, implying that he doesn't have to look. Bill Harford's cluelessness throughout this film is discussed in more depth in my poetry book *handholding: 5 kinds*, second edition, Kore Press, forthcoming in 2020.

liii.   In an interview, actor Bradley Whitford stated that that Jordan Peele may have incorporated this line into the script because Whitford said this in all sincerity in real life. https://news.avclub.com/bradley-whitford-didnt-realize-get-outs-obama-line-was-1835163054,

liv. I'm indebted to writer/editor/publisher Steve Cannon for introducing me to this term. He was describing Sekou Sundiata's writing excellence to me once by saying "He can *pen*."

lv. I'm indebted to poet/visual artist Christopher Stackhouse for initially introducing me to this fact about Poe.

lvi. "Wraiths and Race" article in the *Guardian*, Dec. 02, 2002. https://www.theguardian.com/books/2002/dec/02/jrrtolkien.lordoftherings

lvii. ""

lviii. It also has the capoeira aspect of appearing to be something unassuming (Black folks dancing) when it's really a strategy for survival (graceful martial arts technique from Africa). In retrospect, I was using Poe's work to marshal my own internal imagination, to see the universe and myself differently than I was told to see my environment, me.

lix. "Village Ghetto Land," song by Stevie Wonder, Tamla Records, 1976.

146

lx. We are seeing the inside-out version of this now with the opioid epidemic and its sympathy for its victims that is different now than it wasin the 1970s. The scourge of this new versino of this epidemic affect populations that are now majority White in the U.S. Racism is a perverse/inverse factor in this: "…what I believe is happening is that racial stereotyping is having a protective effect on non-white populations." https://www.npr.org/2017/11/04/562137082/why-is-the-opioid-epidemic-overwhelmingly-white

lxi. http://web.newworldencyclopedia.org/entry/Blood_libel is an example of this thinking.

lxii. *The Stoop* was also the name of a short-lived yet important publication/workshop helmed by Steve Cannon and John Farris (circa 1990–1993).

lxiii. In a July, 2019 conversation with my brother John about this experience, he reconfirmed that they played as if they were the characters, not superimposing themselves, including their Blackness, *onto* the D&D characters.

lxiv. In addition to specifically cultural Blerd performativity/Black speech acts, I'm also referring to theorist/theater artist and Performance Studies founder Richard Schechner's distinction between make believe and make belief here.

lxv. I'm referring to the *Family Matters* (television show), created by William Bickley, Michael Warren. Miller-Boyett Productions, Bickley-Warren Productions, 1989–1997.

lxvi. From the HBO comedy special *Delirious*, starring Eddie Murphy, 1983. There are some who say that he lifted the premise of the joke from Richard Pryor. My understanding is that many comedians, especially pre-internet, appropriated central themes from others.

bxvii. *She's Gotta Have It* (television show), created by Spike Lee, 40 Acres and a Mule Filmworks, 2017.

bxviii. This is even more explicitly the case in the second season of the show that had been recently released as of this writing. In that season, on a visit to Puerto Rico, Nola directly connects to and does artistic renderings of ancient African spirituality. A more extensive speculative fiction-based series that considers the Hoodoo-based metaphysics of African culture, and its hybridized forms, can be found in the excellent multi-book, multi-thread fiction series by Daniel Jose Older.

bxix. The hip new Black millenials' t-shirt that says "I am my ancestors' wildest dreams" and variations on this theme, is true in that we/they dreamed that we would simply survive when they knew they would not.

bxx. I'm indebted to Ron Eglash's seminal book *African Fractals* for this idea in African cosmology that I'm applying to the life of the mind here.

bxxi. Prince was also adept at putting overtly political messages within a musically and sexually free context: *Party Up!, Controversy, Sexuality, Sign O' The Times* are examples of this "shapeshifting."

bxxii. Now that everyone on Eearth has seen *Endgame*, I can say that much is forgiven with that incredible entrance they gave the Wakandans in the last big battle scene. It was certainly a befittingly regal, Black po re-introduction. approach.

bxxiii. The Wakanda story reminds me of 19th century China being forced to open up to the West after the devastation of the Opium Wars. The West caught up (technologically—using the Chinese innovation of gunpowder) and came in with a vengeance (literally). I guess *Black Panther*'s writers are saying: better to open your doors on your own terms.

bxxiv. *Ghost,* film directed by Jeff Zucker, Paramount Pictures, 1990.

bxxv. And now even more open in anoother realm himself. RIP, to the legend-maker Stan Lee. A great artist and a good guy, by most accounts. He really tried to make the worlds he wanted to see. Maybe that"s why he connected to so many of us, and we to him.

bxxvi. *New York Times*, 01/20/2018.

bxxvii. This is pure speculation on my part but it"s the only thing that makes sense since, in the future, there only seems to be one of us around at any given time.

bxxviii. MLK Jr. was also a Blerd in more ways than one: He was obviously a human rights policy wonk, a student of philosophy, a religious scholar, and a wordsmith. He was also a hardcore Trekkie, as Nichelle Nichols relayed to Reddit: https://www.washingtonpost.com/news/arts-and-entertainment/wp/2015/07/31/how-martin-luther-king-jr-convinced-star-treks-uhura-to-stay-on-the-show/?utm_term=.e803482879a7

bxxix. Lordy though, I could see why they kept a shirt on him for most of the series, he was hot as *hell*. The three leading men could not compete with ripped flyness of Takei. Real talk! The episode, btw, was called, perfectly, "The Naked Time" (TOS: Season one, episode four).

lxxx. I recently watched these scenes again and they age very well. They were really pushing the sexual envelope with those moments, especially for the time.

lxxxi. Saw this episode again recently and still… nope. Btw, the episode is called "Plato's Stepchildren" (*ST: TOS*, Season three, episode ten).

lxxxii. Look at about a dozen "Blaxploitation" film fight scenes around that time and you'll hear a very similar vocalization. A combination of the type of Black vocalizations one hears in traditional fight scenes of the 70s are presented by Michael Jai White in the parody film *Black Dynamite* (2009). This type of voicing is a form of performative utterance that would not seem to meet the premise of Austin's concept of locution, that it "make sense." This almost glossolalic/onomatopoetic subset of utterances in martial arts (whether because of formal training or not) serves as illocutionary force (conveying the martial force of the fighter) as well as perlocutionary force (that the listener/opponent received the intention of that force to intimidate, announce, warn, etc.). It would not, in Austin's schematic, meet the requirement of locutionary force (that the "word" had a particular meaning) but it meant something to the person on the other end of it. .

lxxxiii. Film *The Karate Kid*, directed by Harald Zwart, Columbia Pictures, 2010.

lxxxiv. Musician, composer, clothing designer, and activist Fred Ho incorporated politicized and hybridized versions of these cultural interplays in his work. Another interesting and surrealist intersection of African and Asian diaspora cultures is in the delightful and innovative animated series *Tuca & Bertie*. Created by Bojack Horseman veteran Lisa Hanawalt, the two leads are voiced by Tiffany Haddish and Ali Wong. Although not overly racialized (they are playing animated anthropomorphic *birds*), the performative utterance of their voices, as well as the fact that people recognize the voice actors' names and how they look in real life, does have some racial reference for the viewer/listener. In this series, the focus seems to be more on gender solidarity (across species and kingdoms, including plants) than ethnic commentary.

lxxxv. Exemplified by the opium wars in China and heroin and crack epidemics here in the U.S. and, likely now, the opioid crisis.

lxxxvi. Behabitives, in Austin's framework, are performatives that reflect social behaviors, agreements, etc.

lxxxvii.　I am aware that subsequent scholarship has illuminated problematic statements by Gandhi. However, King clearly wasn't emulating those ideas and there's no indication that he was aware of them. Also, I mean, if I can repurpose Edgar Allan Poe's value despite his pro-slavery stance, I can certainly note Gandhi's fundamental importance to MLK Jr.

lxxxviii.　*Daughters of the Dust*, film by Julie Dash, Kino International, 1991.

lxxxix.　I've had great conversations with my former grad student, dancer/

performance artist O'Neal regarding water and Black aesthetics in dance.

xc. *Akata Witch* (novel) by Nnedi Okorafor, Viking/Penguin, 2011.

xci. References for this riff: Priest/scholar John Mason in conversation with the author regarding the concept of coolness and water in the Yoruba-based belief systems circa 1992 ; Miles Davis recording *Tutu* 1986, Warner Brothers Records; Archbishop Desmond Tutu, anti-apartheid clergyman and activist 1931– present, whom the author met briefly at Hunter College circa 1992; and the three etymological speculations on the apparel in Wikipedia (not usually a primary source for me but insightful for the purposes of this comment).

xcii. I've gone parasailing, hot air ballooning, and skydiving to engage with this aspect of the lizard brain as research. I found it liberating to do so. The last two junkets were while I was writing a book, so that may have helped…anything to take a break from that task and "clear my head." lol.

xciii. Much later, a member of the collective Brooklyn Hi-Art! Machine, Deborah Kass, extended this omnipresent New York reconfiguration of "Yo" with her outdoor installation piece OY/YO in front of the Brooklyn Museum, adding the Yiddish-originated phrase "Oy" into the visual texture of the word "Yo." The installation was accompanied by large public art pieces by the two other members of the group, Kameelah Janan Rasheed and Hank Willis Thomas.

xciv. One could count the *Black Lightning* tv show introduction of heroine Anissa Pierce, Black Lightning's oldest daughter, as a "descendant" of baby Mike Evans' character. In a more gendered, queered, and Latinx context, the character Mel in the new reboot of the tv show *Charmed*, I suspect, owes her confontationalist comments, especially to her Wwhite lighter Harry to early Mike Evans dialogue. As far ask I know, his was the first young character, with his bold, topical revolutionary statements and corrections, on television.

xcv. Or, as Prince might say: dance, music, sex, romance, in the song "DMSR," from the album *1999* (Warner Bros. Records, 1982).

xcvi. Both legendary Norman Lear's tv creations from the 1970s.

xcvii. This is based on a conversation I had the pleasure of having with Caz himself when I ran into him at the Rock 'n' Roll Hall of Fame, Cleveland, Ohio in September, 1999.

xcviii. Several media outlets have noted this, including AM New York in an interview with Grandmaster Caz. July 12, 2017. https://www.amny.com/entertainment/the-1977-nyc-blackout-and-the-hip-hop-spark-that-ignited-soon-after-1.13796834

xcix. Misfires as voided statements, etc., including Austin's example of a cat being on a mat and under the same mat simultaneously, one "christening" a ship without the authority to do so, etc.

c. The "good times" cat went from being on to under the mat, to riff off Austin's example here.

ci.   We see the same framing being used right now to rationalize the physical and psychological torture occurring at the southern border of the U.S. These vulnerable populations are being seen as "illegals" who don't feel the pain of infant imprisonment, abuse, and separation.

cii.   This also implies that we are of the status of *all* non-humans or, in fact, are beneath them. This is the existential crisis Paul D suffers while considering the rooster "Mister" in Toni Morrison's novel *Beloved* (Alfred A. Knopf, 1997), for example.

ciii.   Even then, I was not interested in identifying with the female characters of *LoTR*. I didn't see myself as Galadriel (the most compelling), Eowyn, or Arwen, but as Aragorn, Frodo, and other male characters.

civ.   Audio file: Cornfield Holler/Cornfield blues Powell, Abraham, performer 05-20-1939 https://www.loc.gov/item/lomaxbib000302/

cv.   Susan Stewart, *Poetry and the Fate of the Senses*, University of Chicago Press, 2002, p. 14.

cvi.   Art Rosenbaum, Editor, McIntosh County Shouters, Folkways Recordings, 1984, liner notes, p. 4.

cvii.   I am greatly indebted to Sekou Sundiata for many things, including his creation of this term.

cviii.   As noted by Fred Moten in his book, In the Break, University of Minnesota press, 2003 re: Saidiya Hartman, *Scenes of Subjection*, Oxford University Press, 1997.

cix.   Jay Hawkins, *I Put A Spell On You*, single, Okeh Records, 1956.

cx.   Nina Simone, *I Put A Spell On You*, single and album, Phillips Records, 1965.

cxi.   This is beautifully and succinctly stated in the currently popular Black phrase "put some respeck" (a.k.a. respect) on one's name when one says it. In a sentence it would be something like: "When you say my name you betta put some respeck on it." Even though the central word is often corrected with a "t," the hard "k" sound is more effective for the type of emphasis being conveyed. It's usually said as a demand, not as a request. In other words, it's meant to sound "hard," not refined. This even works with a slightly softer version of the "k" sound, as seen in the brief, and pointed, interview between rapper Birdman and the morning show radio team "The Breakfast Club" on 4/22/16. Source: youtube

cxii.   Delany and Morris email correspondence excerpt, 10/13/2015. This was based on a discussion of composer Julius Eastman's work and the controversial titles of his compositions. Further comments on this aspect of perlocution will be discussed in the second and third books in this triptych.

cxiii.   This term has now, because of this factor of Black appropriation of a word that has literally killed in its performative utterance, become wholly something else. Earlier this year (2019), I heard a Black woman on the F train angrily curse out a White man (arguing over space in the subway car), a "white nigger," as in: "You white niggers coming in here thinking you can take over" (or something to that effect). She said this unironically and without emphasis on the word "white." While a less common choice, this indicates that the use of this term has been separated from its original racially specific moorings of attack toward Black people exclusively (or Black adjacent) depending on the circumstances of the insult *when a Black person is saying it*. Another, very different meta-commentary on this idea was famously used in a section of a skit created by comedian Dave Chappelle, "Clayton Bigsby: The Black, White Supremacist" when the (blind) Bigsby character misidentifies White youth playing Black music in their car (and presenting Black affect in their mannerisms and clothing). After Bigsby hurls a racial epithet at them, they confirm to each other that he had and take it as a badge of honor about their cultural authenticity (especially as it was coming from a Black person).

cxiv. An excellent example of this contrast/situation can be seen throughout Season one, episode one of the FX television series *Atlanta,* written, co-produced, co-directed by, and starring Donald Glover. Also starring Zazie Beetz, Brian Tyree Henry, and LaKeith Stanfield. The episode aired 09/06/2016.

cxv. The commentary that I used for Prince being a "free Black man" or a "free man" was inspired by the presence of Mr. Delany as well as my conversations/correspondences with him over the years.

cxvi. Interestingly, this issue was addressed in a slightly more subtle way early in the *ST: TOS* episode "The Savage Curtain" at the 12:03 mark.

151

cxvii. Or even more pointedly, as a substitute for "this m*****f***** over here," with all the potential for irony, humor, sarcasm, political commentary, and play implied by a comedic delivery.

cxviii. Austin uses the terms "felicitous" or "happy" interchangeably for performative utterances that work as intended. He moves away from the idea of true/false binaries. Rather, he uses "infelicitous" and "unhappy" to frame failed speech acts.

Also, I find it interesting that when I have heard this comment said by White people it has not *hurt my feelings*. It fails as a behabitive for me, even though the term doesn't resonate for me in a complete 180 as Delany's analysis asserts it does for many Black people. The epithet is just weird and unpleasant, but, I think through my socialization, it has lost some of its power to "kill" in my mind. It has no power *over* me, or most of those I know. When I thought more on the intention of this mean term, what came to mind was a great Black expression for matters that intend to harm, are acknowledged as such, but fail in their power: the racist utterers can "kiss my Black ass." This phrase switches the performance intended to do harm and offers…another type of performance for the utterers to do.

cxix. This comment is also a reference to the creation of African American Congolese-based charms that use knotting as referenced in Robert Farris Thompson's book *Flash of the Spirit*, in chapter two. Source: *Flash of the Spirit*, First Vintage Book Edition, August, 1984.

cxx. Reference to the chorus from the song *Formation* by Beyoncé Knowles, Parkwood/Columbia Records, 2016.

cxxi. In Austin's commentary in *HTDT*, behabitive utterances are statements of social interactions, feelings, etc. Other terms referenced in this context are phonemes—the sonic building blocks that words (or sounds with specific shape and meaning) are built upon, phatic acts or phemes, utterances that have a vocabulary base—usually words—and rhetic acts or rhemes, words with a specific reference in mind.

cxxii. See above.

cxxiii. This is a "riff" off of the concept of *minkisi* (spiritual packets) developed by Congolese people and their descendants. This is referenced extensively in Robert Farris Thompson's book *Flash of the Spirit*.

cxxiv. This metaphor references *Flash of the Spirit* and particularly Thompson's referees regarding Congolese spiritual knotting.

cxxv. The issue, the complaint that Black folks often make about appropriation of our Black bodies, our Black selves, our Black creations, is because our existence is not affirmed in the making, not because we aren't generous with our genius.

cxxvi. What I'm also saying is we can't abandon these touchstones of Black culture and then get mad when folks be bitin' (to be mean) or are simply inspired (to be kind). The Blues, Rock 'n' Roll, Doo Wop are just some musically-based utterances that have been at the fulcrum of this discourse. We honor those who went before us to not dismiss the old school for another new thing. We have to hold on to both the old and new as a source of pride.

cxxvii. I mean, I have to say this since I try to make everything about *Brooklyn*.

cxxviii.　　　Even less so after visiting his grave in Accra, Ghana. I mean, if anything, Du Bois' magnitude is very much *understated*. He had strategic plans set up for his life comfortably *past his 100th birthday.hundred* He was not playing! He had set very high standards for himself as well as his service to others.

cxxix. I was literally "putting my hands where her eyes could see" (to repurpose the genius Busta Rhymes), Black Casper in her racist mind: a friendly, colored, *ghost*.

cxxx. I don't assume that only Black folks will read this but, taking my own advice previously stated, that doesn't mean I can't make the focus of this manifesto the community/communities that I'm from.

cxxxi. The "Negress" term is a reference to the *ST:TOS* episode I mentioned in a previous footnote.

cxxxii. In the second season of Spike Lee's tv show *She's Gotta Have It*, the Jameelah Hawkins character, portrayed by Ciera Payton, shows how this plays out in the non-academic corporate world. It's not *just* academia, but people often ascribe loftier values to ivory towers.

cxxxiii.   The exploitation and manipulation of graduate students and non-tenured (especially part-time/adjunct) faculty, as well as those who are staff who teach, are blatant examples of unfairness in academia, as many reports have attested. Faculty of marginalized groups are even more vulnerable.

cxxxiv.   The false equivalency arguments by those who feel their success must come and is predicated on the expense of the currently/formerly aggrieved don't hold, especially in this context. And if the "classics" are so great, can't they stand up with the great work of others?

cxxxv. It's also true that as a young college student, everyone who's a teacher seems established, ubiquitous, powerful. Little did we know how exposed both of these departments were at the time and how vulnerable those new faculty members were. I also failed to appreciate how strongly each department was tied to its activist roots.

cxxxvi.   Two examples of these excellent formative teachers are Drs. Richard Valcourt and Andrew Polsky. A cursory google search of their activities since I left school indicates that they both may have veered much more to the right over the years. (I guess they'd say I veered much more to the left…) At any rate, *at the time* they each affected a heretofore unknown Blerd interest that I still have, an amateur fascination with public policy and how governmental agencies work. I had no idea I had Blerd tendencies in this area until I went to Hunter College. Blerds *love* learning new things! Writing this now, I'm reminded about how enduring these insights by different types of professors can be, even if we later, strongly, disagree. This aspect of learning is when academia truly meets its promise.

153

cxxxvii.   Prince's relationship to his own hair was peek ""Black woman"" level variety.

cxxxviii.   Just ask the late Jacques Derrida. In his book *Limited Inc.* he spent some time throwing shade at philosopher John Searle for not deserving to sit at the big kids table. Derrida will cut you! Lol. It also means that even though Derrida had another point of view, he took Austin very seriously as a philosopher.

cxxxix.   As the critic and theorist Marjorie Perloff has noted, I'm embarrassed to say, I mention being a Gemini a lot. So I'm just straight up owning it now! I have no reason to be proud but I do beam a bit at these two giants being twinsies.

cxl. Uttered line in the single lp song *Slave to the Rhythm*, sung by Grace Jones, Island Records, 1985.

cxli. And could certainly apply to the extraordinary, luminous Harlem visual artist *Grace Williams*.

cxlii. *HTDT*, p. 145.

cxliii. *The Good Place*, created by Michael Schur, NBC, 2016. I have hopes for this tv show but am cautiously optimistic. We've had disappointments with riveting, balanced Black characters before. See my comments on the tv show *Good Times*, as well as the ultimately very disappointing Fox tv series *Sleepy Hollow*, among others.

cxliv. There are also featured Black performers throughout the show, including Bambajan Bamba, who's in a significant number of episodes, but there is no Black *community*. The great Maya Rudolph portrays a character called The Judge, who also notes that she is perceived as a Black woman on Earth and how hard that designation is to navigate on Earth. In the flashback scenes to Chidi's life on Earth, there seems to be more of a connection to Black folks in the aggregate. Another thing I credit the show for is the effortless way they state African names, rather than exoticize/problemetize/nickname these words.

cxlv. Although fantastical in his own mysterious geeky way, I also have to shout-out Greg Morris (no relation) from the old *Mission: Impossible* tv series as the stoic (and too often off-camera) Blerd.

cxlvi. One could argue that in this way he is a more light-hearted version of the fictional character Elesin in Wole Soyinka's play *Death and the King's Horseman* (W.W. Norton, 2002).

cxlvii. Riffing here on a line from the film *The Devil Wears Prada*. The Miranda Priestly character, performed by the superlative Meryl Streep, says: "Everybody wants this. Everybody wants to be us."

cxlviii. At this point I'm reminded of police brutality victim Rodney King plaintively stating "Can't we all get along?" The infelicity of this utterance, particularly at the time that he said it, is remarkable as a statement "devoutly to be wished" by him to the point of feeling fictional, or like a play.

cxlix. She is an absolute force of nature as a live performer and has long presented as non-binary/genderfluid/androgynous. When she was the featured star of Afropunk in 2015, and especially their "fancy dress ball," Black folks turned out for her—in all ways—*resplendently*. Her charming book *I'll Never Write My Memoirs* (Grace Jones with Paul Morley, Gallery Books, 2015) comments throughout about her international scope and regular returns to Jamaica to commune with Rastafarian friends there.

cl. Ms. Jones found hers the hard way, through an abusive childhood and during the course of her being at the trailblazing front lines of innovative art.

cli. A beautiful way to articulate some of these ideas might be through the long prose poem by Khalil Gibran, *The Prophet* (reprinted by Vintage, 2015). In the section on Joy and Sorrow, he writes: "Then a woman said, Speak to us of Joy and Sorrow./And he answered:/Your joy is your sorrow unmasked./And the self same well from which your laughter rises was oftentimes filled with your tears." Another example, one of my favorites, are the Baby Suggs performative utterances for her people in the Jonathan Demme-helmed film of Toni Morrison's classic novel *Beloved*. Featuring the luminous Beah Richards as Baby Suggs, people found their freedom *through* the body as her utterances urged them on, in a double refashioning.

clii. Both literal and colloquial (Hip Hop-focused) meanings.

cliii. I note the performance artist Jaguar Mary X here, for her work in glossolalia..

cliv. Excerpt from Mos Def's song "Umi Says," from the recording *Black on Both Side*s,

Rawkus/Priority Records, 1999.

clv.   This is a common trope in speculative fiction tv shows where the scientist/bookworm/investigator either can't believe what's going on magically or can't help much because they're out of their depth in the face of it. In the tv show *Grimm*, for example, the police acumen of the leads helps somewhat but often only to cover up the magical nature of crimes. *Charmed* stands out from these more traditional constructs in this and other ways.

clvi.   The research on these African-based belief systems matters is fairly lightweight in the scripts, and the writers, although earnest, clearly *skimmed* in these areas, but it's more logical that the three charmed women being Latinx and two of the three identifying as Black in the show and in real life would also seek out culturally relevant magical solutions, not just ones based on European Wiccan systems.

clvii.   If I didn't know better I'd wonder if she was from Brooklyn! High praise! Actually the actor is British, from Nottinghamshire. She's a Gemini (*coincidence*? lol. yes. iIt absolutely is a coincidence.). To tell the truth, the first thing I noticed when reading about the *character* was that she shared a birthday with Jimi Hendrix and Bruce Lee. Her character is between the two ages of both of these men when they died. This is very likely a coincidence but I'd prefer to say kismet!

clviii.   Even when the Mel character gets mad salty towards men and patriarchal oppression to uber-snarky levels. She is the representation of the proudly feisty grad student/young scholar. My teacher side hopes the character goes back to complete her graduate education. I'm willing to serve on her dissertation committee... lol.

155

clix.   Notably co-produced by Jordan Peele.

clx.   Not only is this a great metaphor of the character, I"m adding this here because it"s important to note how intellectual ability even in a ""non-intellectual context"" is empowering. People *want* to feel smart and are smart, in an array of environments.

clxi.   Haddish herself has had a harrowing and extraordinary life, thatwhich I learned a bit more about after I'd already written this book. She is truly an exceptional "o.g." to navigate so many hostile environments, including speech act environments in her home, in foster care, and with intimate partners, according to her autobiogaphy, *The Last Black Unicorn*. Gallery Books, 20179.

clxii.   For example, there's a great scene where Shay's husband, Josh Birkeland, gets in the face of one of the other White parents who used what has historically been considered a racial epithet when used by Whites. (Season two, episode two.) He's protecting his Black daughter. The show does a great job showing the newer complexities around language and code-switching.

clxiii.   The authors here seem to have a stronger grasp of these traditions than the writers in *Charmed,* and it is reflected in clearer writing about these ideas in context. It is noteworthy though that these very different series go to the same "roots" as a natural outgrowth of having Black women characters as leads in shows that connect to magical-spiritual utterances in some way.

clxiv. And to bring it back to Austin's problem with this binary construction, the representation is "doing" as much as it is presenting something "describable," just as Nola's process in making the art can be described but can fail to capture what she "does."

clxv. Reference to the 1964 Carl Lerner film starring James Whitmore, produced by The Hilltop Company. Based on the 1961 book by John Howard Griffin.

clxvi. A poem by Miguel Algarín by the book of the same title. Scribner, 1997. This is arguably the best book title in poetry, in my humble opinion.

clxvii. Mos Def, from the song "Umi Says." See previous notation.

clxviii. As I said in my intro to my bilingual poetry book *Per-Form/Hard Kore*, my preference to either/or is usually "both please." Joca Seria Press, Paris, 2017.

clxix. One of my favorite African American phrases. (I'm not sure if it's been gentrified, or even originated outside of Black spaces.) There's a particular mellifluousness that I've heard when this phrase is uttered, usually a bit stridently, but sometimes not, reflecting the temporal Cartesian finessing by the "souls of Black folks"—to riff on W.E.B. Du Bois (again) for a bit.

clxx. He uses the idea that if a cat is on a mat, the cat isn't logically under the same mat at the same time. It's a mutually exclusive situation.

clxxi. I'm using "not Black"" and "non-Black" subtleties here as phrases for clarity and to also dislodge the habit of ""othering"" Blackness and defining Eurocentricity as the only standard.

clxxii. An example of this subjectivity "on the flip side" is discussed in an article in *Scientific American* called "White Nationalists Are Flocking to Genetic Ancestry Tests—with Surprising Results," with the tagline: "Sometimes they find they are not as 'white' as they'd hoped." There was an interesting note in the article about the overt subjectivity of race that was purely illocutionary (performance based on a particular intent): "Other [white supremacists], he said, responded to unwanted genetic results by saying that those kinds of [DNA] tests don't matter if you are truly *committed* to being a white nationalist." [emphasis mine] *Scientific American*, August 16, 2017. Once again, Dave Chappelle proves to be ahead of his time.

clxxiii. It is worth noting that Teena Marie could've easily ""gone the Elvis route"" and been cynically appropriative with her great voice and Black vocal affect. She would''ve likely been very wealthy had she chosen to. I don''t know what went into her decision -making to be marketed/seen as a ""strictly R&nB"" singer, but I have no doubt that it was a conscious decision: Mmodern Black music is replete with examples of long-standing and one-hit- wonder White artists that have been appropriative *and* bigoted/envious of Black music. They then enhance their careers at a certain point by calling themselves something else or making their non-Black affiliations explicit in some way and disavow the Black communities that helped to launch their careers.

clxxiv. One of the brutal and hilarious takedowns of Timberlake's fraught status as appropriator was presented by the parody web series *The Legends Panel*. Youtube:

(*PARODY*) *The Legends Panel: Whitney Houston's Return and Justin Timberlake*, published April 13, 2013. *The Legends Panel* and I share lingering "feelings" about the Super Bowl fiasco and Timberlake's less than stellar response. We got you, Janet—Ms. Jackson ('cause we "nasty").

clxxv. Katt Williams, the legendary comedian, did a great riff on the proximity of African Americans to Chicanos/Mexican Americans as vulnerable political classes in his most recent Netflix stand-up special, *Great America*, 2018.

clxxvi. "Manipulate (someone) by psychological means into doubting their own sanity."— Oxford English Dictionary online.

clxxvii.　A great explanation of individual gaslighting from a feminist lens that can be applied to racially charged situations is the *Everyday Feminism* article "10 Things I've Learned About Gaslighting As An Abuse Tactic," August 27, 2015, by Shea Emma Fett https://everydayfeminism.com/2015/08/things-wish-known-gaslighting/

clxxviii.　Sometimes this is literally the case, unfortunately. Too many examples to mention here but trust me, it's true. It's worth its own entire book. I want to make it clear that I don't find anything dishonorable about working in service industries. (I have family members who have done so.) However, in the situations I'm describing here, the presumption is that we are all in the same social stratum but the personal interactions underscore that we are not. I think highly of the work of visual and conceptual artist Michael Bramwell in this regard. A bit more on him later in this chapter.

157

clxxix. This can also be a weird thing for a Blerd because many of us are acculturated to be "problem solvers" of some sort. This is particularly the case in higher education, tech industries, and middle-upper management contexts.

clxxx. The people whom I've encountered, or whose work I've encountered, who seek radical social change take these consequences very seriously and don't make statements regarding such lightly, if at all, because they are *doing the work*.

clxxxi. Unfortunately, after Austin's death—a meeting between these two personages would've been an extraordinary encounter.

clxxxii.　Malcolm X's extraordinary connection through metaphor between the performance of violence and the performance of language is worthy of separate study in speech act theory. Source Youtube: https://www.youtube.com/watch?time_continue=2&v=v3Ffhedw5IY

clxxxiii.　In Ella Baker's case, her text was transformed into song by the activist a cappella group Sweet Honey in the Rock and has subsequently been covered by others. Although Sweet Honey in the Rock has a uniquely stellar reputation for doing this type of work, it is also part of a long-standing African American tradition to convert text to song, as a mode of expressing aspects of liberation movements. A notable example is the sacred musical thteater of the Ring Shout, mentioned earlier, that does with song (and movement) what capoeira in Brazil does with dance and martial arts: use one aesthetic form to belie the liberatory work undergirding it.

clxxxiv.   The intentional gaslighters, etc., do not need my help, you know? Be better people, deliberate gaslighers., be better.

clxxxv.   Actor/writer Danny Hoch is doing the Lord's work as the most obviously obnoxious Hip Hop-focused example of this type of person in the tv show *She's Gotta Have It* as the character Dean "Onyx" Haggin.

clxxxvi.   "…that part of the individual's performance which regularly functions in a general and fixed fashion to define the situation for those who observe the performance." Erving Goffman, *The Presentation of Self in Everyday Life,* Anchor Books, Doubleday, 1959, p. 22.

clxxxvii.   And even sometimes, for all those efforts and all that preparation, it doesn't work. For instance, the tragic, untimely, and unfair death of twenty-nine-year-old conflict resolution mediator Anthony Baez. https://www.democracynow.org/1996/10/22/police_brutality

clxxxviii.   Austin references Hamlet's advice to the players frequently in *HTDT*, as well as other literary notions. With Hamlet, Austin usually refers to "suiting the action to the words," but I thought this line was also apropos. My Shakespeare riff on his riff.

clxxxix.   I should clarify to say at least *not as much* overt minoritarian status—the gendered "softness" of the protagonist is a factor in the surprise tension that's built.

cxc.   Although I think her Scottish accent here is an indicator that she does not in fact belong with the RP speakers at the party and the class they underscore. I'm indebted to many of the people I encountered in visits to Scotland in 2018 for these insights, as well as poet/scholar Shelagh Patterson for the development of my observation in this regard.

cxci.   Another well-known and not so small-scale example of this is Marlon Brando's 1973 refusal to accept his Oscar at the Academy Awards ceremony that year. He sent Sacheen Littlefeather as a proxy to reject the award on his behalf and to advocate for Native American rights in film.

cxcii.   From the Crystal Waters *Surprise* album, Mercury Records, 1991.

cxciii.   My first experience of Mr. Bramwell's work was in a gallery. He was sweeping small squares of tile, wearing a generic maintenance uniform, in the gallery. I spoke to him immediately—not knowing he was performing art at the time—because he was one of the few Black people present at the downtown art gathering I attended and because I tend to speak to people in service industries out of habit. (They are often ignored/objectified as an assertion of racial and class-based prestige in these settings.) Mr. Bramwell performs this type of work all over the world, including in Goree Island, Senegal, and Hiroshima, Japan, as well as in African American communities. A review of one of his pieces early in his career in Harlem was written by the Associated Press on 9/11/1995: "Artists [sp] Turns Art Into Life With A Broom."

cxciv.   Another example that's a little out of the scope of the postscript writing is the musician Lizzo. In addition to being an extraordinary singer/rapper/flautist/dancer, her writing and empowering of one of the most marginalized and stereotyped group of people, large dark-complexioned Black women, is highly charged and very political. To not only assume her own facial beauty (she is stunning), but her body's beauty (she looks healthy, curvaceous and strong) as well as her decision to move her strong, healthy beautiful body and to show it moving and shaking, as it naturally would do, without shame, is a complete reversal of the societal "norm." She has put this in the context of other marginalized people in her writing and the casting choices of her videos. She's using her artist privilege to reinforce the respect and joy she associates with the range of Black female bodies. Her recent collaboration with the great artist Missy Elliott (the song "Tempo") underscores that Lizzo sees herself in the transgressive tradition of Black women embracing self-pride, sexuality, and love of our bodies irrespective of what dominant society deems the norms to be at any particular time. I would hasten to add that in many Black and Brown communities (whether heteronormative or Queer), the beauty and eroticism of larger women has long been established and continues to be assumed. This has been the case in this country as well as globally.

cxcv. I've had very helpful conversations with my former grad students performance artist/ scholar Julie Dind and , as well as activist, theater artist, and scholar Catherine James regarding neurodiversity and performance,.

cxcvi. I'm taking a bit of liberty with Austin's use of the term here.

cxcvii. Toward the end of HTDT, Austin generously and wisely says: "Here, then, is an instance of one possible application of the kind of general theory we have been considering; no doubt there are many others…Moreover I leave to my readers the real fun of applying it in philosophy." *HTDT,* p. 164.

cxcviii.   As it so happens, this was right around the time of Prince's death.

cxcix. This is a riff off one of Stevie Wonder's lyrics in the song "As": "When you say you're in [the world] ,but not of it/You're not helping to make this earth/a place sometimes called *hell*/Change your words into truths/And then change that truth into love/And maybe our children's grandchildren/And their great grandchildren will tell…" Stevie *always* has a phrase for the right occasion. I guess there's a pun intended here if you know the song…

cc. This book's creation is obviously engaging with it.

cci. Why do films like *Terminator* and *2001: A Space Odyssey*, make us feel as though we have to choose between the two? What I like about the first *Matrix* film is that it makes us feel as though we have a chance to struggle for this better world as/with technophiles.

ccii. **Probably not how Austin would describe it. lol.**

About Tracie Morris

Tracie Morris, MFA, PhD, is an artist and theorist from Brooklyn, New York. She is currently the inaugural Distinguished Visiting Professor at the Iowa Writers' Workshop. This is a significantly revised and expanded version of her 7th book, which was also published by Chax Press.

About Chax

Founded in 1984 in Tucson, Arizona, Chax has published more than 240 books in a variety of formats, including hand printed letterpress books and chapbooks, hybrid chapbooks, book arts editions, and trade paperback editions such as the book you are holding. From August 2014 until July 2018 Chax Press resided in Victoria, Texas, where it was located in the University of Houston-Victoria Center for the Arts. UHV has supported the publication of Since I Moved In, which has also received support from friends of the press. Chax is a nonprofit 501(c)(3) organization which depends on support from various government private funders, and, primarily, from individual donors and readers In July 2018 Chax Press returned to Tucson, Arizona, while maintaining an affiliation with the University of Houston-Victoria. Our current address is 1517 North Wilmot Road no. 264, Tucson, Arizona 85712-4410. You can email us at chaxpress@gmail.com.

Recent books include *The Hero* by Hélène Sanguinetti (transl. by Ann Cefola), *Since I Moved In* by Trace Peterson, *For Instance* by Eli Goldblatt, *Towards a Menagerie* by David Miller, *The Long White Cloud of Unknowing* by Lisa Samuels, and *Io's Song* by Murat Nemet-Nejat. You may find CHAX at *https://chax.org/*